AN
OF
AND HER
GENTLEMAN

AN OFFICER AND HER GENTLEMAN

TWO AVIATORS
TWO COCKPITS
ONE JOURNEY

MANDY + CRAIG HICKSON

First published in UK in 2025

Design: Burge Agency
Cover portraits: Holly Bobbins
Cover photos: Jamie Hunter and
James Penberthy

A CIP catalogue record for this title is available from the British Library.

ISBN: 978-19-1931-291-0

www.mandyhickson.com
Facebook @MandyHicksonSpeaker
X@MandyHickson
Instagram @mandyhicksonspeaker
Linkedin @Mandy Hickson

Linkedin @Craig Hickson
Instagram @hickoc320

ABOUT THE AUTHORS

Mandy Hickson is one of the Royal Air Force's first female fast jet pilots, flying Tornado GR4s on frontline operations. After nearly two decades of service, she has become a highly sought-after keynote speaker, delivering powerful lessons on decision-making under pressure, leadership and resilience to global businesses and organisations, from FTSE 100 boardrooms to schools and charities. Mandy is a trustee for the RAF Charitable Trust, has served as an Aviation Ambassador for the Department for Transport, and is an Ambassador for Girlguiding. She is also the author of the bestselling memoir *An Officer, Not a Gentleman* and continues to inspire audiences with her candid reflections on breaking barriers and thriving in high-stakes environments.

Craig Hickson served as a Royal Navy helicopter pilot, flying anti-submarine missions and later moving into search and rescue. He retrained as a fixed-wing instructor, teaching military pilots on aircraft including the Hawk, before transitioning to the commercial airline sector as an Airbus A320 captain. Craig went on to become an instructor and examiner, training pilots from all over the world. He believes there is greatness in everyone, some find it themselves, many need support and encouragement from others. His chance came when the Royal Navy gave him an extraordinary opportunity to do something worthwhile. Known for his calm, thoughtful approach to leadership and his ability to get the best out of people, Craig brings decades of aviation experience and a unique perspective on teamwork, decision-making, and resilience.

DEDICATED TO ALL THOSE WHO DARE TO DREAM, FACE THE TURBULENCE... AND KEEP FLYING ANYWAY.

ACKNOWLEDGEMENTS

From both of us, our sincerest thanks go to Rob Hodgetts. Your talent, patience, and uncanny ability to bring our stories to life have been the glue holding this book together. You've taken two very different voices, countless anecdotes, plus more than thirty years of experiences, and somehow woven them into one coherent journey. We are endlessly grateful.

To our proofreaders, Amanda, Sarah and Lynette, thank you for your excellent advice and guidance and for following the perfect debrief.

Over the decades, we have been lucky enough to cross paths with so many people who have shaped, supported, and inspired us. From schoolteachers, to the RAF and Royal Navy, from friends and colleagues to those we've met only briefly but who have left a lasting mark, thank you. You've each been part of our journey in ways you may not even realise.

Mandy: To my Mum and Dad, Sue, Sarah and Frances, your belief in us has been the bedrock we have built everything else on. Thank you for listening, for encouraging, and for always being there for us.

Mum, you are the strength behind everything I do. Your example from my earliest memories are of courage, kindness and determination. Your sage advice has guided me through every stage of my life. You taught me what it means to stand tall (very tall), to weigh myself daily, to keep going when things are hard and to always look out for others along the way. When I grow up, I still want to be just like you!

Dad, I know you are no longer here in person, but I learnt so much from you. Your resilience and determination, how to cry in public, how to eat a curry, how to swing a golf club and how to drink a pint with ease. I feel your presence always and love you so much.

Sarah, you are not only my sister but one of my greatest friends. Your humour, honesty and loyalty have always lifted me and made the good times even brighter. To have someone who shares your exact sense of humour, to roar with laughter and quote Victoria Wood endlessly to, I could not imagine this journey without you by my side.

Fran, I love the way of friendship has developed so much, they say tough times bring you closer and however sad this was, at least it has brought me closer to you.

And to my incredible friends, the Birmingham Bezzas, my Kili crew, Club (we had to ditch the word 'book'), Summer Starjumps, The Flamboyance of aircrew, the spin girls, the Winchester collective and everyone else in between, thank you for being there through every high and low, the well-timed humour and the fantastic celebrations when we had something to cheer about (all too often). You reminded me to laugh out loud when things felt too serious and to keep going when I've been on my knees. You are all part of the crew that got me to this point. Thank you.

Craig: To my loving Mum and Dad. You continue to inspire me; I feel your support and thank you for encouraging me to live my life to the full. Mark, Vanessa and Paul, my amazing brothers and sister. You have influenced me more than you know and I continue to seek your guidance. Thanks to Roops, my best buddy. What a top man you are. You were there when I needed you most. So many laughs over so many decades.

To my Brighton buddies, Navy chums, Airbus colleagues, Winchester mates and everyone else who made my life so interesting and fun, thanks to you all for your enduring friendship. It is all of you who have made the real difference to me over the years.

And to each other: we've been wingmen for over half a lifetime now, in more ways than one. To Craig, thank you for being my constant source of humour (yes, you are very funny), for your love and support. You've always pushed me to reach for the skies, and yet you ground me when I need it the most. To Mandy, what a life we have had together. In any description it has been bonkers, crazy and full of adventure and excitement. Life just keeps on giving and long may it continue. You are my universe, and I love you more than ever!

Finally, and most importantly, to our fabulous children; Elliot, Chessie, Jack, and Jamie. We encourage you to live your lives in your way. In a way that is fulfilling, meaningful and inspires you to seek as many experiences as possible. We love the fact that you are all following your hearts, travelling to far flung places, grabbing every experience that life throws in your direction. You have made our lives infinitely richer. We are so proud of you all and we love you so much.

CONTENTS

Prologue		13
Chapter 1	Mission brief	17
Chapter 2	Take off	29
Chapter 3	Climbing through the clouds	49
Chapter 4	Levelling out	77
Chapter 5	Turbulence ahead	109
Chapter 6	Buzzing the tower	163
Chapter 7	Your captain speaking	193
Chapter 8	Navigating change	213
Chapter 9	Aerobatics	227
Chapter 10	Final approach	249
Glossary		263

PROLOGUE

Laid out in the story arc of a flight, this book is designed to take you on a journey. We start with a mission brief, then move through take-off, climbing through the clouds, cruising at altitude, hitting turbulence, pulling off aerobatics, and finally landing before planning the next mission. This structure is not just a creative choice. It mirrors the way we have lived and learned, both in uniform and in the years since leaving the military.

Although many of the stories we share come from our flying and military careers, this is not a chronological autobiography. We dip in and out of different periods of our lives, weaving together the moments that best illuminate each theme. Some come from the cockpit, some from the classroom, some from raising a family, and others from running businesses and working in completely different sectors. Our aim is to show that the lessons we learned in high-pressure environments are not limited to aeronautical roles, they are just as relevant in everyday life, whatever your profession or stage of life.

We take you on a fictional flight, using each phase to explore a key theme, illustrated with examples and stories from our own lives. Before take-off, we conduct our pre-flight checks, making sure all the switches are set, and everything is ready to leave the ground. Figuratively, that is your status as you open this book: where you are right now, on the threshold of change.

Taking off, we face into the fear of failure, that gut-clenching moment when you push away from the comfort of the runway, and explore the power of controlling the controllables. As we climb through the clouds, we tackle self-doubt and imposter syndrome, those inner voices that whisper "you do not belong here," even though you have done the hard part and got airborne.

Once at our preferred altitude, we level out and take a breath and look out of the window to the horizon. This is where we examine how to create the right environment for yourself and others to thrive and why choosing your reaction to life's situations is a superpower only you have. But turbulence is never far away, and we use this phase of the flight to look at the bumps and threats in everyday life and career, the moments that can knock you off course and put you into what aviators call an Undesirable Aircraft State.

In 'Buzzing the tower', we examine threats of our own making, those times when, like Maverick, we push the limits, or when we simply make mistakes that can spiral into bigger problems. What matters is not avoiding every error, but how we respond and recover.

Leadership, for many, is seen as the ultimate destination, but in 'Your captain speaking' chapter we explore why it is less about reaching a position of authority and more about the way you lead yourself and others along the way. Navigation, another crucial pilot skill, becomes our lens for decision-making and dilemmas. We know how easy it is to tie ourselves in knots searching for the 'right' answer. Here we offer strategies to break the cycle and navigate through life with less stress and more decisive action.

And of course, flying is not all pressure and procedure. There is joy too. Aerobatics, with their loops and rolls, remind us that we all need moments of exhilaration and play. We use this phase to talk about flying high, honing your skills through debriefs and reflection, and challenging the system when there might be a better way forward.

Finally, every flight must come back to earth. We bring our fictional journey to a safe landing, ready to refuel and set a new course. Where you go next is entirely up to you.

This book is not about becoming a pilot, but it is about learning to fly in your own life. By the time you turn the final page, we hope you will feel better equipped to face turbulence, more confident in your ability to navigate uncertainty, and ready to take off towards your next adventure. I know with certainty that there are many awaiting us.

CHAPTER 1

MISSION BRIEF

MANDY: All pilots are superheroes. Especially the fast jet lot with the sunglasses and the swagger. Except they are not. They're just like you or me.

Granted, I was a fast jet pilot in the RAF, but I was still Mandy from Manchester who was first told I had an obesity problem and couldn't join the military, and then went on to fail my aptitude tests to be a pilot. And even then, after proving time and again I could actually fly, was only taken on as a test case to see how far I could get before I failed. Talk about cultivating the perfect breeding ground for imposter syndrome. Still, I managed three tours of Iraq and was only the second female RAF pilot to fly combat missions in a war zone.

Cruising through a velvet night towards Baghdad with ribbons of red tracers from anti-aircraft guns streaking into the sky like fireworks, knowing surface-to-air missiles are trying to lock on to you, is quite the ride, I can tell you. More fun – mainly because the locals aren't generally trying to shoot you down – is flying a fast jet at low level through the valleys of Wales or Scotland, rocking left and right as the curves of the hills wrap around you like a blanket, screaming along just 250 feet above the ground. That's the height of a pylon, by the way.

But superhero? Not really. I sat at the pointy end of the aircraft, a Tornado GR4, with a navigator in the back seat. We were very highly (and expensively) trained in those jobs, but many people are equally highly skilled in their chosen profession. Sure, we had some attributes and competencies which enabled us to get to that point, but I was still me, with all my imperfections and doubts and worries.

After countless sorties into the darkness and light of Iraq I would be back home in the UK buying milk and bread in the supermarket like everyone else.

Even the uber-confident Maverick from the *Top Gun* movies eventually realised it wasn't all about him and that he had to rely on others in his team.

I met Tom Cruise, the actor who played Maverick, at an airshow once. He was on a publicity tour to promote the release of *Top Gun: Maverick*, the sequel to the 1986 cult classic. I was there as a host and ambassador, interviewing aerobatic display teams and astronauts. One day I wandered into the patron's tent where I spotted Tom in a roped-off section with the head of the RAF, Air Chief Marshal Sir Mike Wigston, or 'Wiggy' as I knew him.

Wiggy was my squadron executive officer in Iraq, and he called me over.

"What, me, come and meet Tom, no, it's OK, are you sure?"

None of these words went through my head. I was in there like a sharp-elbowed shopper on the opening morning of the Oxford Street sales.

I'm not generally one to get star struck as people are just people to me, but as I walked over, my adrenaline surged, as if I was pulling a 4G turn in the Tornado with my G-suit punching me in the guts. Rather conveniently, Wiggy took the copy of my book *An Officer Not a Gentleman* which I was clutching and thrust it into Tom's hands as he introduced us. I immediately suffered what in aviation terms would be described as a loss of directional control of the mouth and began blathering on to Tom about how much I loved him and his films and how instrumental *Top Gun* was in fuelling my career fantasies.

It came out the year I joined the air cadets, so was the mental backdrop and soundtrack to my early flying experiences. I knew all the lines and practised all the moves in the cockpit, and it sparked my dream to fly fast jets – although it really was only a dream for me then as women weren't allowed to be pilots in the RAF. Wiggy showed Tom some photos from my book of him and I on operational duty in Iraq, and Tom flashed that famous smile from beneath his aviator shades.

"You guys are the real-life heroes. I'm just an actor," he grinned.

Just another normal lunchtime then. How I wished I'd recorded that as my ringtone for my phone. We chatted for a few minutes about flying and my time in Iraq.

He was very complimentary and very humble. As far as I know he still has my book. Maybe he's writing a film script as we speak.

An Officer Not a Gentleman tells the story of my time at the vanguard of women as combat pilots in the RAF and talks about my initial obstacles, such as gender-biased pilot tests, to imposter syndrome, being described as 'Amazonian' and not feminine enough during officer training, the pressure of life at maximum capacity and casual sexism on the front line. For all that, it was my dream job, and I loved almost all of it. The flying was spectacular, and the laughs and stories will last a lifetime. For much of it, I tried to fit in as one of the boys and probably changed my behaviour accordingly, drinking too much, swearing too much, dressing in a navy blazer and beige chinos like the rest of them when we travelled abroad.

It's a good topic for debate. Why was I acting like this? Should I have had to? Isn't that just part of being a team player or was I losing my authenticity? There are numerous shades to it, but the truth is, having women as pilots in front-line squadrons was new to everyone and we were all learning as we went along. My book ends with a story about a young air cadet called Emily, who had all the skills to be a fabulous pilot but really needed to believe in herself. As an instructor I'd taken her up for a flight and made the classic mistake of judging a book by its cover, thinking this uncommunicative, sullen teenager was one more half-hearted student to get through before I could clock off for the day.

Grunting and monosyllabic as we got under way, her flying turned out to be a revelation. What I didn't mention in the book is that at the end of our first flight together, she said: "I want to be just like you."

Just. Like. You. That was the catalyst for me.

My RAF career was coming to an end as I chose to have a family rather than go back to flying on the front line. The RAF, in its infinite wisdom, said I wouldn't progress any further if I stayed in a desk job. So I was grudgingly heading towards the classic airline pilot route because let's face it, what else was I good at? But Emily made me stop and think. Really think.

Did I want to follow every other military pilot – such as my husband Craig, a Royal Navy flyer, for example – into the itinerant life of a commercial flyer? And how were we even going to manage that with two young boys at home? Emily's comment sparked a chain reaction, and although I passed all the exams to fly commercially, I opted to leap into the unknown and took off on a different, and at first, far scarier route. I now talk to businesses and institutions about my experiences, explaining how I tackled the challenges along the way and offering employees some insights into how they can apply a few of these learnings to their own development.

To offer a different perspective for this book I've collaborated with Craig, my husband, a former helicopter pilot turned fixed-wing instructor, fast jet pilot, commercial airline captain and training captain. Craig's very different to me. He's a thinker and will dwell on something for some time, while I move on almost instantaneously. I don't do regret, I think it's a futile emotion.

He's a meticulous planner, the sort of person who has to make sure his suitcase is all packed and sitting by the door the morning before leaving for a trip. By nature, I'd whack some stuff in a bag that day, although his ways are rubbing off on me. I'm loud and an extrovert, Craig is generally the opposite, he'd call himself a confident introvert although he definitely has his more flamboyant moments. What's interesting is that we both advanced in our flying careers in different ways and with different qualities.

This highlights the essential point: that there is no single blueprint for a job. Sure, there are skills and competencies to be picked up along the way, but it is possible to arrive at a similar place having taken very different routes. Neither of us were superheroes and we both struggled to get off the ground, let alone navigate a smooth flight throughout our careers. It would be easy to think when you're setting out – or even later in your working life – that only you are facing challenges and that the world is against you.

But dealing with obstacles is supposed to happen, it's the normal course of events.

I was recently at a Trustees board meeting for the RAF Charitable Trust, and a very wise gentleman, a retired army lieutenant general, told a wonderful story which culminated with the phrase, "Setbacks are not stumbling blocks, but stepping stones". It resonated so much with me. Everyone has bumps in the road at some stage. It's called life.

The interesting bit, and what gives it some meaning, is how you embrace these challenges along the way. Craig and I certainly didn't always get it right. And we're not claiming to have all the answers, or even any of the right questions. But if you're searching for a bit of inspiration to turbocharge your own path, wherever you are on that journey, then hopefully we can add a few drops of aviation fuel to your smouldering fire to seek change.

CRAIG: I can't really read. I mean, I can sort of read, slowly, to myself. Eventually I'll get the gist, but it's not what you would describe as fluent reading. If you asked me to read out a chapter of this book, I'd go a bit red, panic slightly inside, mangle the first few words and then give up.

I'd be having flashbacks to English lessons at my school when I was asked to read out a passage. I'd point at the words, stumbling over each one as I tried to assemble the letters into something understandable, hoping I'd luck out and get it close enough that there would be no titters and I could move on to the next one, like a game of Articulate. When I kept mucking it up, the smirks became snorts, building to hoots and guffaws as the clown sitting next to me fed me the wrong words on purpose. Even the teacher would join in the laughs.

Kids are kids and I get it, it was probably quite funny for them, but for me it was a disaster. I would spend all week dreading English. I became so preoccupied by this, so petrified of being asked to stand up and read that I didn't really have the head space for anything else. Each time it happened I would be mortified, shrinking with embarrassment.

I felt so small, so insignificant. Ashamed, I suppose. I told the teacher, but he just said to practice reading. Not exactly genius advice.

My writing isn't much better. I found physics OK and I was acceptable at maths. I played for the school tennis team and even represented the county, so I wasn't a lost cause but once you get a label of dunce attached to you it can be poisonous for your own growth. I just got increasingly demoralised.

It's not that I didn't back myself or even like myself. I was happy enough around people and I've always found it easy to connect with others. It's just that I thought I was daft, worthless, thick. So did the authorities, by the sounds of it.

In my school report just before sitting my O'levels the headmaster had written: 'I hope he gets through, but I shall waste no pity on him if he fails. His future is quite clearly in serious jeopardy. In not one single academic subject is there any real evidence of a proper attitude.'

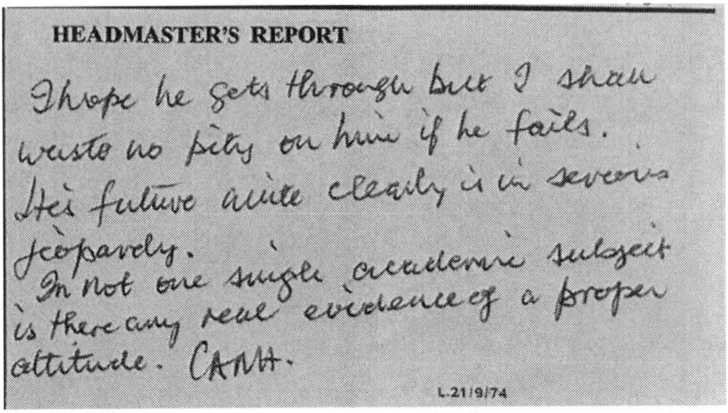

HEADMASTER'S REPORT

I hope he gets through but I shall waste no pity on him if he fails. His future quite clearly is in serious jeopardy.
In not one single academic subject is there any real evidence of a proper attitude. CAMH.

L.21/9/74

I'd already failed my 11-plus exam to get into my older brother's school and then I couldn't wait to get out of my all-boys secondary school. I hated it. I ended up with an unclassified grade in my English O'level which basically means I offered nothing worthy of scoring a mark in the exam. Not that I would recommend flunking exams, but this little titbit has given me endless pleasure over the years as a shock tactic to spice up dinner party conversations.

I left school at sixteen and I remember having an interview with the headmaster, who told me I'd done really badly and wouldn't be welcomed back. Honestly, I left his office thinking what an idiot he was. I used to wish I was like my little brother Paul, a clever git who never struggled in lessons or exams. But then my career might have taken a completely different path.

All of our children struggled at school in some form or other and they'd come home and say, "Dad, I can't read" and I'd think, well neither can I. When our middle son was eventually diagnosed with dyslexia and ADHD, the penny finally dropped. That must be my problem too. There wasn't much analysis of this sort of thing in my day and no labels to attach to things.

Name Hickson C.

House Hakelweare **Age** 15-8

	Set / Posn.	
English	C 24/24	A poor term and a disappointing 'mock' result (34%). His approach is much too 'light-hearted'. P.Y.B
History	B 25/27	Neither his 'Mock' exam nor his term work gives me much reason to expect him to obtain an 'O' Level pass this year unless he makes a very big effort now. W.F.A.
Geography		He has passed at "O" Level & is using the periods for extra work on other subjects. RSB
French	C 14/15	Certainly not one of his better terms. His 'Mock' result was poor – little sign of preparation was evident. He works in class, but this is not enough. DCJ
Religious Education		A very satisfactory term's work. As a Confirmation candidate, he contributed well in discussion. RJC
Extra Tuition		

Form V B

Average Age in Form 15·10

Subject	Set / Posn.	Remarks
Mathematics	Set B Posn. 14=/21	On occasion his work can be very good indeed but unless he can sustain some measure of consistency in his work he may not pass his 'O' level! SR
~~Ex. Maths.~~ Physics ~~Ex. English~~	B2 13/13	His 'mock' examination was extremely poor and he has done very little, until the very end of term, to make up for it. I am sorry to see an able boy throwing away his 'O' level chances. [illegible]
Biology ~~Latin~~ ~~Metalwork~~	B 19=/20	The mock 'O' level demonstrated how superficial and patchy his knowledge really is. Without a lot of serious work NOW he hasn't a remote chance in the summer
~~Art~~ Chemistry ~~Spanish~~	B 14/22	RHC Fairly able boy, but rarely takes his work seriously. Needs a greater commitment if he is to succeed. P.J.W.
Project		Forestry He has shown interest and willingness this term. W.J.F.
Other Activities		

Maybe it would have helped, maybe it wouldn't. It might have offered some explanation for my continued failings, but then again it might have offered a convenient excuse for others to block my path and curtail my ambitions. I still don't read for fun, in fact I've never read a novel in my life, apart from *An Officer, Not a Gentleman*, for marital reasons, obviously. I used to be embarrassed by my reading level, but in my mid-fifties I decided I didn't care anymore.

I've learned a few things along the way though: about how to manage and motivate yourself; how to treat others; how to excel in your chosen path and navigate change; how to deal with setbacks; and not least, which buttons to press, levers to pull and pedals to push to get a multitude of aircraft into the sky and bring them back down safely. I've never set any goals, never had big dreams to be prime minister or an astronaut or whatever. I don't know what I'm going to do in five minutes, maybe I'll have a cup of tea. Big bold goals ('The Plan') work for some people, for example Mandy, just not for me.

My path has not been uniform or consistent. There have been many failures and I've journeyed down different routes. But equally, it hasn't come about by accident or luck. It's been structured and I've given it thought at the right time.

After my early struggles at school and several false starts, I eventually became a helicopter pilot in the Royal Navy. I did a stint in search and rescue and became a fixed-wing instructor, flying a host of aircraft including the Hawk, the jet of Red Arrows fame, my favourite aircraft of all time. When I left the navy I switched to the commercial sector, flying the Airbus A320, my second favourite aircraft. I moved over into the captain's left-hand seat and then became an instructor, training pilots first on the line during the course of their day jobs and then as a type-rating instructor and examiner.

Nowadays it's the teaching and the human behaviour aspect that fires me up. It has been a fun ride, but it has not been easy and there have been plenty of downs and difficult days. I've often been asked how I manage to luck-out with my various jobs. In the military it is because I regularly contacted the appointer, suggesting the job I thought I would be good at.

I would send a full covering letter laying out all my skills, competencies and why I was the best fit for the next job. Don't ask, don't get is the old saying, but it's true in the world of work as much as it is in life. To me, life is like an escalator, or more accurately many escalators heading in different directions. I want to keep moving.

I'm happy to switch escalators now and then. Sometimes they might swing about a bit or slow down but as long as I'm trending in the right direction, that's OK. To where? I don't know.

It's all about the journey, not the destination.

So, while we won't be dishing out any flying lessons in this book, we will be sharing a few of our experiences to show how we navigate through the turbulence of life. Hopefully, we can stimulate you to think in a different way and challenge yourself to achieve your own personal greatness. And if I end up having to read passages aloud to an audience because the book has been a roaring success, it will be well worth it.

CHAPTER 2

TAKE-OFF

MANDY: What superpower would you choose? Some people like the idea of being invisible, others the full Dr Who time-travel thing, or the ability to read minds. Flying is a popular one and would be great fun, leading to some mad adventures. But what if I gave you a superpower that made you immune to the fear of failure. Think about it for a bit. No longer shackled by self-doubt or wracked by worry about what might or might not happen.

No longer thinking how it might feel if you mess up or it doesn't quite pan out the way you wanted it to. There would be none of that trying to second-guess an outcome or stressing about what-ifs or shying away from a challenge. No worries about leaving your comfort zone, or being embarrassed, disappointed, maybe even humiliated.

As humans, we tend to be governed by emotions. Often, the fear of failing is more powerful than the thought of succeeding. We sometimes protect our ego by constructing a narrative for why we are not putting ourselves out there. We're all guilty of it.

It's too easy to just convince yourself that maybe it's not right this time and take the easy option because the thought of failing doesn't sit well with your sense of pride. It's like sitting in an airplane cockpit on the runway. The engine is running but the brakes are on, the throttles closed and the switches off and you're not going anywhere. But instead, imagine you are armed with this anti-fear-of-failure superpower helping you ease off the brakes and open up the throttles.

With this protective shield, you now run towards opportunities and grab them vigorously, embracing all the challenges along the way and growing from them as the waves of fear just crash off you and wash away. It might be that you push yourself to go for that promotion, or you apply for that new job you've seen which feels like a bit of a stretch, but you'd love to do it and maybe, just maybe they will see your potential. It might just be that you try new things in your current position which could lead to new opportunities and growth. And at the very least it might banish the nerves and jitters ahead of a meeting or a big presentation or an interview.

The trouble is, no such superpower exists, at least not available off the shelf. Most of us have to cobble together some makeshift armour of our own to fight through challenges, whether it be fear of failure or fear of change. I often explore this superpower with the younger audiences I speak to, but it doesn't grab their attention in the same way that, say, being able to fire spider webs out of your hands might. But that's because they haven't accumulated any of the baggage or insecurities of the adult world and realised how powerful it would be to have no fear of failure.

Recently, I was watching an artist performing on the stage at the prestigious Pendulum Summit, a leading business and leadership convention in Dublin. He asked the audience of about 3,000 people to stand up if they were an artist, or even considered themselves good at art. About ten brave people stood up and declared their talent to the world. The speaker then said that when he asked audiences of primary school children the same question, they would all leap to their feet.

So, why as adults do we feel constrained by the fear of failure, or of not being good at something? We put ourselves into the proverbial box, in this case, "I'm no good at art". Which is daft anyway, because art is subjective.

Emily, the student I talk about at the end of *An Officer Not a Gentleman*, had been unenthusiastic, monosyllabic and seemingly completely uninterested at the start of our flying lesson. When I told her afterwards that she was one of the most talented pilots I'd ever flown with at a basic level, she was completely blown away.

She opened up and said that she was so scared she was going to fail that she decided not to try.

Sheryl Sandberg, the former chief operating officer of Facebook and then Meta, wrote a fantastic book called *Lean In*, which tackles women's anxieties about reaching the top. But it's not just women. As humans we have a tendency to lean out, which creates a buffer, our protection zone. Another high achiever Sir Richard Branson advocates saying yes to opportunities and then figuring out how to actually do the task later.

Then there is the England men's cricket team, which has lately developed a style of play known as 'Bazball' after the nickname of their Kiwi coach Brendon 'Baz' McCullum. Epitomised by star player Ben Stokes, it is about playing with a positive mindset and creating opportunities, both batting and in the field. It is playing without fear with everyone backed to the hilt. If you get out trying to take the game to the opposition, so be it.

The idea is that unshackled by thoughts of failing, looking unworthy or inadequate or getting dropped, the players can thrive. They've had plenty of success with it too, although there will always be doubters questioning a new way of thinking.

Knowing when to lean in and when to take a wider strategic look first, is the key for us as we look to alter our paths. People often say to me they wanted to be a pilot or wanted to join the military but never did for various reasons. I wonder whether being scared to fail was a contributory factor.

I now like to call it the 'I could have done this if I'd...' You fill in the blank. If you can try to work out what your '...' is, then you can try to work out what is holding you back from achieving your goal. The key here is to be totally honest with yourself and examine your reasoning.

Voice it to others if it helps to expose the flaws. It's not that you won't still fail occasionally, but at least you won't be held back by the fear of failure in the first place and will be giving yourself the best chance of maximising your potential.

I'm a firm believer in controlling the controllables, and your own mindset is the one thing only you can control. Sure, events and people can influence it but you're ultimately in charge. You can choose to be scared, anxious, offended, belittled or whatever. Or you can choose not to.

If you can't control it, let those thoughts go. But if you hold yourself back and don't try, imagine how many opportunities might be behind that door that you didn't lean on or peer around, just to see. It's the law of unintended consequences – that different paths throw up different opportunities that you couldn't have foreseen back at the crossroads. When I left the RAF without a firm plan, I couldn't even have imagined I would end up hosting the Pendulum Summit in front of thousands of people but that's just a consequence of hopping onto a different path.

You can't know what's down the road so embrace the adventure.

The smart way of looking at setbacks and failure is that they are necessary. They are part of the journey. In a weird way that's the fun bit because that's where growth comes from. And by the way, every single one of us goes through struggles, despite what social media might have you believe.

Embracing the uncertainty and engaging with the struggle rather than fighting it are the power moves. Or, at least, that's the sort of lofty idealism that abounds in podcasts and on myriad social media posts. It's not always as easy in practice.

When I started my first desk job in the RAF after leaving a front-line flying squadron I had a two-hour commute each way from Winchester to High Wycombe. On the first day, I trudged up the stairs to the new office in slow motion with a sense of doom pressing down on my shoulders and a cannon ball of dread in my stomach. What the hell have I done? This is not me. This is awful.

It's easy and convenient in hindsight to say you should cheerfully embrace those moments when your mojo is missing and your inner voice is telling you this doesn't feel right, but it's very hard at the time. Your gut instinct is a powerful force. But by starting small and even just acknowledging you're in a 'discomfort' zone you might be better able to reframe what you're going through.

I knew this was the start of my transition from Tornado pilot to a more normal life for the benefit of my family, but it didn't make it any easier. I was clinging on to my comfort zone of G-force, Mach speeds and machismo. It might not feel like it at the time, but each little period of struggle is building experience, filling that pool of resilience and arming you with antibodies to fight through the next curveball life throws at you.

Think about toddlers trying to walk. There's a lot of huffing and puffing and falling over and tears, but they all get there eventually.

In the military they train repetitively and intensively to build layers of experience. Train hard, fight easy, as the saying goes. That's why at each stage in my training to be a fast jet pilot, I had to fly up to 100 sorties on each aircraft type, from mastering the basics, to learning to fly against other aircraft in air combat, each with increasing complexity to build up the learnings and add to that pool of resilience. That allows you to handle the knocks and gives you the reassurance you'll cope better next time, which breeds confidence.

And confidence plus purpose equals resilience. It becomes a self-sustaining system if you manage it right.

CONFIDENCE + PURPOSE = RESILIENCE

My biggest early failure could have been terminal. After an intense day on the computer screens at the Officer and Aircrew Selection Centre (OASC), RAF College Cranwell in the heart of the flat lands of Lincolnshire, I was told I'd failed the RAF's aptitude tests to become a pilot. Apparently, my skills at keeping a little green dot in the middle of a screen using a control column and pedals or manoeuvring a blob through a maze were not up to scratch. That's even though I had my private pilot's licence to fly real aircraft, and I'd won trophies for aerobatics as a student pilot at the University of Birmingham Air Squadron.

Failing your aptitude tests to be a pilot is clearly not ideal if that's the career you've got your eye on, and I sobbed all the way home. My future was in tatters, I felt ashamed, rejected, but also indignant. My boss at the air squadron was sympathetic and as confused as I was. He arranged for me to be assessed by two independent instructors, who both said I was more than capable, in fact, above average.

He said I shouldn't lose heart and would be allowed to take the tests one more time, I clung onto that as a lifeline.

I then received a letter offering me a bursary to become an air traffic controller with the RAF. Good on one hand, but on the other they didn't even see me as a navigator. They had me down for a non-flying role. Cue more howls and tears.

The boss lined up the second test and I went down to OASC full of hope. It's OK, you'll be fine, obviously there was some mistake last time, maybe you were just a bit off. I came back bereft after failing again. The boss advised me to accept the RAF's offer while he worked on my case in the background, so I turned up for officer training at RAF College Cranwell as a very reluctant air traffic controller.

He reasoned it was better to fight the system from within.

It's a good example of being willing to get on an escalator going in roughly your direction and put your best efforts into that, so you're ready to jump onto another one going in exactly the right direction if the chance comes up. And then bingo. A few weeks into the course I received a letter in a simple brown envelope explaining I'd be switched to pilot. So much heartache, disappointment and sleepless nights but now I had the golden ticket to my dream life.

Behind the scenes the boss had been hard at work and convinced the RAF bigwigs that the tests were not designed for the way a woman's brain works. He even uncovered an unconscious bias that meant a much higher percentage of men passed the tests compared with women. Much later I discovered they had only agreed to take me on as a test case just to see how far I got in pilot training before I failed. But I always had a funny feeling that it would work itself out, and in my head, I saw myself as a pilot.

Even though I didn't appreciate it at the time, failing the aptitude tests and, before that, being told (wrongly, as it turned out) that I was too overweight to earn an RAF flying scholarship to university – and losing three stone (unnecessarily) to achieve it – were building up my resilience to setbacks. Both were driven one hundred per cent by purpose. I was desperate to fly and join the RAF as a pilot, so fighting the urge to reach for the biscuits to get that scholarship was quite easy. But they were also fuelled by a sense of injustice, that the system wasn't fair and had let me down through no fault of my own.

My motivation has also been linked to this idea of 'Don't tell me I can't'. Everyone's motivation is different. Find yours and use it.

We saw this panning out with our son. In his late teens, as he had decided not to go down the academic route any further, he decided to set up his own business. It started at a small level, buying products at a competitive price from wholesalers, having them delivered to our house, repackaging them, sticking a barcode for Amazon on them and then shipping them off directly for Amazon to sell from their warehouses. It's called Amazon FBA if anyone fancies looking into it.

The business grew enormously; he ended up hiring a warehouse space and occasionally employing friends to help fulfil his orders. When he needed to register as a Limited Company to become a business and become VAT registered, he quickly realised why he had been so profitable, because he was making twenty per cent more profit than his competitors due to the fact he had been under the VAT threshold. He persevered for another year, but we could see this was getting increasingly difficult. He kept on telling us that he had failed, but all that we could see was how much he had learned.

He was now twenty years old, had set up limited companies, had worked and negotiated with other businesses, had mentored eight others in how to set up their own business (aged from 17–65) and had changed his teaching style completely for each mentee. He had also submitted accounts and VAT returns. His learning curve and problem solving was phenomenal. How could he see this as a failure? When he then decided to close the business down, he demonstrated quality decision making, sensing it was time to get out.

Failure is only the case if we do not learn from the experience, and he had learnt so much.

After I left the RAF, I was severely lacking in mojo, feeling a little lost, with no sense of identity. One Friday evening over dinner with friends I was recounting a flying tale from RAF days and everyone seemed gripped. Either that or they were being polite as it was my house and I was supplying the wine. One of the guys at the table was Harvey Thorneycroft, the former Northampton and England A rugby player who runs an events, consultancy and speaker business with his wife, and my close friend, Alice.

When I had finished regaling everyone, Harvey said that was just the kind of stuff his audiences would lap up and asked whether I had considered speaking at corporate events. No, because I've never been to one, I replied. In fact, he said, they had something coming up at Brocket Hall in Hertfordshire which I would be great for. They wanted someone to talk at a conference for top-level insurance executives about decision-making under pressure and risk taking.

It all sounded fairly doable, and the wine was flowing so I accepted.

I prepared copious notes, wrote numerous cue cards and practised for weeks for the big day. With a few deep breaths and a pounding heart I gave my speech and it seemed to go down OK. Afterwards I asked Harvey what he thought. "The tales were great Mands but ditch the bloody notes. It's your story, you can't get it wrong."

I felt a bit deflated, like the time during officer training at RAF Cranwell when I was picked up for clicking my tongue seventeen times in a three-minute presentation. I asked Harvey if there were any of his other speakers I could watch for some tips, so he took me along to an event with Alan Chambers, an ex-Royal Marine and polar adventurer. Alan had the audience on tenterhooks with some brilliant anecdotes and lessons; all delivered off the cuff without notes. Afterwards Harvey introduced me to Alan, and I asked if he had any advice for a budding speaker.

"Two words," he said. "Be yourself".

I was hoping for a bit more, maybe some contacts and leads, but I rolled it around my head on the way home and the penny dropped. Be yourself. My brand is me.

Shortly after my rather raw speaking debut I was on a skiing holiday in France and at dinner in the chalet on the first night the chap next to me asked what I did for a living. For a few seconds I was flummoxed. I would normally have responded that I was a pilot in the RAF. It always gave me a glow, and I enjoyed watching it sink in. The eyes would widen; there would be a pause (but you're a...) and then a flurry of questions. But now I didn't have that crutch to lean on. For a brief second I was stumped. I gulped and paused... and then I heard myself confidently state that I was a keynote speaker.

A few seats away, Craig almost choked on his starter.

The guy was a lawyer and he said his firm was looking for someone to speak at an event in London.

"Yes, absolutely, of course I can, that's what I do," I said.

If you say you are and believe you are, then you probably are. Or at least you could be if you stick at it. That's leaning in, right there. It felt empowering.

I was moving on. Positive visualisation can be a powerful tool. I firmly believe that seeing yourself in a role – or even a different mindset – is an important part of the journey to changing your path. I use the mantra 'Dream it, believe it, do it.' It is a catchy way of summing up an idea from the 1903 book by author James Allen titled *As A Man Thinketh* (which in turn he got from the book of Proverbs in the Bible).

It essentially says a person will become what they think they are. I am a strong believer in that. Clearly you can't just think yourself into any job. There might be skills, competencies and knowledge to acquire but seeing yourself in that role in the first place is the start of the journey, as it was mine in yearning to be a fast jet pilot.

Then at each stage, believing you are what you aspire to be, will likely get you there quicker. If you act, think and speak like someone more senior than you, the chances are you will move up the ladder quite quickly.

The military is very good at heaping responsibility on you early and I was often tasked with leading a briefing even though I was one of the more junior pilots. It can be highly nerve-wracking at the time, but it helps paint this picture in your head of you performing at a higher level than your status might suggest. We would also have 360-degree 'wash-ups' after a mission, where everyone's performance was critiqued, from the boss down to the most junior pilot. It is how high-achieving teams' function and it is all about improving collective performance.

Questioning why your squadron boss was late taking off for a mission into Iraq also makes you realise everyone is fallible. It opens your eyes to the fact that actually, maybe you could be in their shoes one day. However, positive visualisation is not voodoo. You have to have the competencies – or, and this is crucial, the potential – to back it up.

If I wasn't good enough for the RAF to spend millions of pounds on my training, I would never have got the chance to switch to pilot, no matter how much I pictured myself in the front seat.

Owning your own story can be powerful in other ways, too. Instead of acting like a victim and saying you've just been made redundant, build a different narrative for yourself. You can't change what happened, but you can control the message you are projecting to the world. I've spoken to people who are still talking about their redundancy many years later.

That chapter has finished, whatever you might think of the ending. It's time to write a new one.

So, before you prepare for your own personal take-off, start with some pre-flight checks of your own. Review your attitude to failure and look beyond the what-ifs. Then make sure the motivation engine is purring, the right mental buttons are pressed, the head switches are in the right position and sufficient confidence juice is in the system to ease off the brakes.

CRAIG: I don't mind the company of guys, but I prefer girls. Which is why Eastleigh College of Further Education was a revelation compared with my all-male school. It opened my eyes to what life could be like. It was so much more relaxed, and I didn't feel threatened or have the feeling that people were just waiting to laugh at me again.

I re-did some O'levels and even passed some, including English language and then moved on to try for some A'levels.

I quickly dropped out of maths because I noticed people were playing cards for money and in my infinite wisdom, I decided that looked more fun than passing an exam. I scraped a grade E in physics and failed computer science, which was great because my plan after that was to go to Brighton Polytechnic to do an HND in computer studies. Despite this minor road bump, it appeared Brighton was still willing to take me. The environment at poly suited me down to the ground – loads of friends, few rules, parties – and I had a great laugh, but once again the academic side was a waste of time.

I failed the exam at the end of the first year and had to re-do the course the following year and then stayed on for a third year to eventually pass the HND, even though for most other people it was a two-year course. It was a major shock to everyone, including me when I passed. I think they just got fed up with me being there. The trouble was, I just wasn't interested in learning about computers.

But what next? Mum and Dad were very good about it and didn't give me a hard time. They just asked me politely what I thought I might do now, probably with a veiled subtext of how long are you going to stay here sponging off us?

I got a job as a hospital porter in Winchester which I really enjoyed. It involved all the grim stuff like moving dead bodies around. I really liked the hospital environment and was pondering going into nursing but then I got a job answering the phones at the Pirelli power cable factory in Eastleigh. While I was there, I applied for another job working in computing for Portsmouth City Council.

Armed with my mighty HND in computer studies, I toddled off down to the interview in my shiny Top Man suit and stumbled my way through a series of technical questions set by a couple of chaps in equally cheap suits. At the end, the lead guy paused for a second, puffed out his cheeks, looked me straight in the eyes and said he honestly didn't think I had any aptitude whatsoever in computers. This was somewhat of a blow, and I began to feel dizzy and nearly fainted. They helped me to the sick bay where I lay down on a bed for a while, just staring at the ceiling and contemplating where I'd got to in life.

Craig, what the actual hell are you going to do? You've got an HND in computer science and they've just said you've got no clue. You are well and truly up the creek, and never mind the paddle, you've barely got a boat. Mate, this is bad.

The only solution to this as far as I could see was to go to America for some fun in the sun with a couple of mates. We ended up in Clearwater in Florida where I landed a job as a pool attendant at a hotel. When the woman running it found out we were all sleeping on the beach she invited us to stay at her house, so we lived there for three months, driving around in her selection of convertibles and having a blast.

Meanwhile, in the real world the Falklands War had kicked off. I don't glorify war in any sense, but I found it increasingly fascinating. The TV images of burning ships and people in the water with helicopters hovering above them sowed the seed of an idea. That looked like a really worthwhile job, saving someone's life like that.

That's it. I'm going to join the Royal Navy. It wasn't such a crazy idea as my dad was an officer in the navy, so I understood what sort of life he had. There was plenty of sport, travel, adventure and opportunities for an interesting career.

It felt like the penny had dropped. When we finally dragged ourselves home, I strode off down to the Royal Navy careers office in Southampton, bold as brass because I now had a plan and was very happy about what I wanted to do.

"Hello, I'd like to join the navy please."

"That's great, what do you want to join as?"

"I want to be an aircrewman, the guy in the back of the helicopter on the winch, all that stuff."

The navy guy I spoke to said I couldn't join directly as an aircrewman, I'd have to first join as a rating, the general lower rank, and then specialise.

"You could be a chef?" he offered.

"Hmm, it's not really my cup of tea," I fired back, pleased with the joke but reeling inside.

Is that it? The end of the road already? Dream over before it's even started? The disappointment must have shown on my face because he asked to have a look at my qualifications to see what else might work. I now had seven O'levels, my E in physics A'level and an HND in computers which was apparently, according to certain members of staff at Portsmouth City Council at least, not worth anything. I'll always be grateful that he didn't just show me the door, because after taking the time to read my CV he said that I had just about enough qualifications to join the navy directly as air crew, so either a pilot or an observer. I thought, well I'm not going to be a bloody pilot am I, I can't read or write.

What does an observer do? According to my new mate in the recruiting office, that was the person who actually fights the aircraft rather than just flying it, like a navigator in the RAF. They are the tactical brains and work closely with the aircrewman in the back of a helicopter. Yes, that's it, that's me, helping the people get out of the burning water and all that. Stick me down for observer.

I went back to working at Pirelli's for a few months and then was called to take the navy's flying aptitude tests at Biggin Hill, an old, now-defunct RAF base to the south of London, where later Mandy discovered she had an apparent lack of flying aptitude. About twenty of us sat at desks in a bare old classroom. Each station had a rudimentary computer and aircraft control column set up on which we did a variety of hand-eye coordination tests, such as keeping a green dot in the centre of a moving screen. Then it was onto some maths, number sequences, visual patterns and verbal reasoning.

My brain was fully absorbed but looking around during one of the breaks I realised I wasn't overloaded. It was intense but I was coping. I didn't feel like I didn't belong, no one was making me look stupid here. Plenty of others looked deeply worried and white as sheets.

After the final session we sat at our desks with only a few murmurs here and there as we waited for the staff to come back in. Clutching a clipboard, the main man stood at the front and began reading out names, pass or fail. Quite a few of the early names failed, and that familiar feeling of impending doom was welling inside me. Here we go, another low point incoming.

As the guy droned through the alphabet, I began formulating a plan for how I would break it to the parents. He got to G and told a bloke called Gregory he'd failed and then it was on to the H-s.

"Hickson. Pass pilot, pass observer."

Blimey. A great surge of elation flooded my body; like I had been plugged into the mains. Bloody great, I've actually passed something for the first time in my life. So, this is what it feels like.

It's good. I caught myself grinning. When he'd finished reading out his list, the chief instructor asked for Hickson to make himself known. My heart banged into my chest and my grin disappeared.

I put up my hand slowly and not to its full extent.

"Follow me," he said.

I knew it was too good to be true. What have I done wrong now? He took me into a side room and closed the door.

"Do you understand that you've passed as pilot and observer?"

"Yes sir, very pleased, sir."

"The point is, Mr Hickson," he went on, "on your application form you've put down for observer only. I must tell you that if you get into the Royal Navy they will only take you as a pilot because your scores and tendencies are greater for pilot. What do you think about that?"

I'm very bloody happy about that, I thought, so I changed my application form there and then to pilot and observer. On the train home, the inside of my head was like a cascading firework as I processed what this meant. I couldn't quite believe I'd actually achieved something. I was going to be a pilot in the Royal Navy.

Maybe I wasn't such a doughnut after all.

To join the navy as a pilot or observer you join as an officer, but to satisfy the brass that you're up to scratch you first have to attend the Admiralty Interview Board (AIB), which back then was at HMS Collingwood in Gosport on the south coast of England. The AIB is three intense days of tests, challenges and interviews where you have to show your mettle as an individual, display potential for leadership and demonstrate you're made of the right stuff to be an officer in the Royal Navy. A big chunk of time was spent in an airy, hangar-style gymnasium where we had to solve a variety of problems, such as getting all your team across an imaginary burning stretch of water in a hurricane using planks, ropes and other bits of gym kit. It's about how you manage the task as a leader and how you work in a team.

No one's perfect but it's the potential and the interaction they are looking for. There were group discussions on various scenarios such as getting a casualty off Dartmoor, where the underlying strategy is to say just the right amount, not too much waffling and hogging the floor, but enough to not appear too shy to speak up. There was also a one-on-

one interview with a psychiatrist, who asked questions like, what do you dream about and how many times have you thought about committing suicide?

While preparing for the AIB I'd spoken to a few people, Dad included, and I reckoned I had enough about me to cope okay with those bits. The part that really worried me was a stint in the classroom writing essays on subjects such as the role of the Royal Navy. I knew this would be my weakness and unsurprisingly, it didn't go that well. At least, I reasoned, there was more to the test than just the academics, or I might not have applied.

I was scared of failing in the sense that I was petrified at the thought of what else I was going to do if it didn't work out, but at least I wasn't so scared of the fear of failure not to give it a go. That's the crux, right there. Sure, if we look ahead, we might be scared of what an unwanted outcome brings, but the key is giving it your best shot in the first place. Often, we surprise ourselves to find out that this is good enough.

We were billeted at HMS Collingwood and after dinner we were encouraged to go for a drink at the local pub. "Just don't get smashed," was the advice from the board staff. On the other hand, if you were known to have spent the night hiding in your room it may not necessarily have gone down well either. The military is a social world and they're after people who fit in.

The key to the AIB was the main interview with two senior serving officers and a headmaster from a local school. The walls of the wood-panelled office were decorated with large oil paintings of historic naval battles and the interviewers sat behind a grand old wooden desk, on which lay a number of model ships. The conversation covered my background and motivation for joining up, there were a few questions on what type of ships the models were, and the headmaster delved into the academics, which for me wasn't a very long chat. All in all, I thought I did OK, I looked them in the eyes (careful not to stare too hard), smiled in all the right places (without looking like a grinning idiot), answered as eloquently and thoughtfully as I could (without rabbiting on) and generally tried to will them into thinking I was just the sort of chap they were after.

The afternoon of the third day was judgement time and I was called back into the interview room to meet with the head of the board. Rigid with tension and slightly shaking, I sat down. He smiled weakly at me.

"Mr Hickson, unfortunately you haven't made the grade to be selected for an officer in the Royal Navy."

Another flunk. Another failure. The tears were welling as I was dismissed. By the time I walked out of the gates of HMS Collingwood big droplets were rolling down my face.

How was I going to spin this one to my poor parents?

CHAPTER 3

CLIMBING THROUGH THE CLOUDS

MANDY: So, you have made your move, you've taken your foot off the brakes and taken decisive action to change your path in whatever way seems right for you now, big or small. You've done the hard part and you hoped you would be soaring, but try as you might you can't seem to get above the clouds. Perhaps a bit of self-doubt is creeping in. Maybe you think you've overreached in your willingness to change, like missing the bottom step in the dark.

Am I really up to this, despite all the clever chat I gave them in the interview? Maybe you're attending meetings where you don't quite have a grip on everything that's going on, or people are looking at you for answers, but you feel like the moment you begin floundering they will see right through you and expose you as a fraud. Maybe it's the change itself that is unsettling you, whether that's environmental, logistical or personal. You're now out of your comfort zone, feeling a bit stressed, vulnerable and a bit discombobulated.

New surroundings and a lack of confidence in your skills are a potent combination for that old enemy, imposter syndrome. The bold will say it's invigorating and life-affirming and it's the only way to achieve growth as looked at through the lens of a self-help manual. Maybe that's the case, but that kind of jolly gee-up is not much use for many of us in the moment as we feel exposed and perhaps feel this sense of being out of our depth. That's a stupid phrase, 'Out of your depth'.

If you can swim it doesn't matter how deep the water is. You can clearly swim to have got this far. Probably all you need now is some refinement of your technique.

Early in my speaking career I was asked by the International Atomic Energy Agency (IAEA) to do a talk in Vienna about cultural change, linking it from the aviation sector to the nuclear power sector. You might not be surprised to hear I haven't got an awful lot of experience in the world of nuclear power. Zero, in fact. I didn't pay too much notice to that, though.

Absolutely, of course I can do it, I replied. I put it to the back of mind and only started to contemplate what the heck I was going to talk about when I began to get correspondence from the United Nations, including a humongous online module I had to complete on things like bomb disposal and hostage situations. I was only going to flipping Vienna.

Drawing on my human factors training, I crafted a twenty-minute speech which I was pretty happy with and set off for Austria ready to take on all-comers. But the shivers of nerves really began as I entered the auditorium, which was filling up with a vast sea of middle-aged white men, many apparently from Eastern Europe and Russia, with armies of interpreters. My legs suddenly felt very wobbly, like a new-born lamb, and my vision started spinning. I suddenly felt very small, little old me in this huge hall.

I started to picture the entire conference witnessing my speaking career implode as I floundered in front of them.

Oh, my days, I'm going to seriously embarrass myself. Mandy, what are you even doing here? Atomic energy, for heaven's sake. Who are you kidding? Well, we're about to find out.

Mandy, you absolute chump. You've pushed it way too far this time.

I needed to act fast. Legging it wasn't really an option, both for the immediate bank balance and long-term speaking prospects, so I scurried off to find the ladies to give myself time to think. Locking myself in a cubicle I sat on the toilet and took stock. OK, you're here because they think you've got something to say, you've flown fast jets for the RAF which none of these people have.

I drew on the handful of speeches I'd made by then and tried to recall the feeling of confidence and acclaim I'd received afterwards. Come on Mands, get a grip. You can do this. I said it out loud to make it real, although technically I whispered to avoid sounding like a lunatic on the toilet.

I thought of the TV show Stars in their Eyes, where the public take on the persona of their favourite pop star and walk through a door, to emerge transformed into their character.

I whispered the catchphrase to myself: "Tonight, Matthew, I'm going to be Mrs Confident Public Speaker..."

Up on stage, peering out from behind my mask of confidence, I listened to the first two speakers and wasn't that impressed. Their delivery was a bit flat, a bit monotone and the audience was fidgety. I could see plenty of people on their phones, which gave me confidence. I knew I could hold the audience better than this.

That's when I realised, I wasn't there by luck, or some unfortunate booking error, I was there because I had achieved some sort of success so far in my fledgling speaking career and they had chosen me out of the thousands of speakers they could have called. The very fact that I was feeling like an imposter was a sure-fire sign I'd made a positive effort to move forward on my path. The issue is that I was still lacking experience in these new surroundings and as we've mentioned, experience builds resilience. The more experience you gain, the further your comfort zone stretches, like a balloon being blown up.

To my huge relief, the talk in Vienna went really well. Not only did nobody fall asleep (always a bonus), but people actually came up afterwards to thank me and say they'd learned something, imagine that. In fact, that single event became a springboard for my speaking career, leading to invitations to speak at power stations and energy companies all over Europe. So, I must have done something right in that vast hall of middle-aged men with their armies of interpreters, or at least I got away with it!

But imposter syndrome doesn't only just afflict people new to a situation.

A few years ago, I was booked to speak to the students at the Oxford University Air Squadron. I'd spent three happy years in the air squadron at Birmingham University during my student days and it's what paved the way for my RAF career, so I was very comfortable with this type of audience. I spoke their language. I'd lived their life.

I prepared an entire A-Z poem on all the different things the squadron and the RAF meant to me. I reckoned I had the evening in the bag.

I took Craig along and we turned up at the very grand St Hugh's College for drinks, me decked out with coiffed hair, evening dress and heels. Milling about in the bar beforehand

I clocked a number of very senior, still serving RAF officers in full No.5 uniform sporting chests full of medals. I knew most of them and was aware they had far more flying, leadership and combat experience than me and had risen far higher in the service. Chatting easily, they seemed so assured, so confident in their own skins, so accomplished.

I felt like a bag of insecurities standing under a single spotlight, with its heat searing my skin. It seemed like the people in the room were spinning around me faster and faster as if I was on a waltzer at the fair, with their voices and laughter amplified and distorted into a grotesque cacophony. I shrank back into myself as I imagined all the officers looking at me, pointing and jeering.

Why are you here? You don't deserve top billing. What can you possibly tell us? We're the real deal, you're just a fraud and you're about to come crashing down.

Leaving Craig chatting, I scurried from the bar and sought sanctuary once again in a toilet cubicle to think things through. I'd done hundreds of speeches by now without a problem, but I recognised what was happening; my old nemesis imposter syndrome was rearing its ugly head again. It was this nagging inner voice telling me I'm not good enough and I'm going to be rumbled at any minute. It was the creeping fear that they'll realise I've been hiding behind a mask of competency whereas the real me was ineffectual and useless and not up to the right level.

It felt like I was living inside a net that was closing in on me. It was classic inner chimp stuff, when one part of your brain takes over and starts firing emotional messages, overriding the rational part, as explained by Professor Steve Peters in his book The Chimp Paradox. Trying to fight it was like a game of whack-a-mole, every time I conjured up a good vibe, the chimp would appear to bash it back down.

I hadn't always experienced imposter syndrome; I'd felt fairly bombproof growing up, but the demands of early adult life, I suspect like for many people, began to chip away at the psyche. Getting into the RAF and then becoming a pilot almost by the backdoor fostered a lingering sense that I was on borrowed time, not quite fully worthy of my place. It certainly put me on the back foot at times and being the only woman in most stages of training and then the first female pilot on II(AC) Squadron also added to that slight sense of marginalisation. It didn't tend to surface at the moments you might think, such as sitting in my G-suit and helmet in the hot oven of a heavily armed Tornado GR4 looking beyond the green glow of my heads-up display about to launch into the Kuwaiti night sky for a mission over Iraq.

At such times, I wasn't thinking, hang on, this has all been a mistake, I'm just Mandy and I should probably get out before you all take off on your bombing mission. No, in those moments I was a highly capable and functioning pilot in Her Majesty's Royal Air Force, about to do the job I had been highly trained for, each sortie adding to the layers of experience I was building, effectively nudging my comfort zone further and further out. Instead, the imposter syndrome would creep into my psyche at other times, like fog rolling in from the sea.

When I returned from my first tour of the Gulf, I was required to complete a Recce Combat Ready course, even though I'd already qualified as Attack Combat Ready and had just been flying operationally. We were officially a reconnaissance squadron, so it was probably right that I completed the course. The problem was, I was absolutely rubbish at reconnaissance. We'd have to identify all these silhouettes of aircraft, tanks, guns, surface-to-air missiles, first in the classroom, culminating in exams, and then over a series of fifteen sorties, each increasingly more difficult, trying to identify objects when flying at 450mph.

I had no idea. They all looked the same to me. You could argue this was just a case of knuckling down and learning, like a kid might have to do with times tables, but for me it went deeper. My mojo was draining out of me quicker than I could top it back up.

I had a genuine sense that despite everything I had achieved so far in the RAF, I was going to spectacularly blow one of these tests and someone would tap me on the shoulder and quietly open the door and push me back onto Civvie Street.

"Thanks for coming, Mandy. Top notch pilot? I think not."

I couldn't shake it and the more I tried to cram the info into my head the more panicky I became. My final sortie was a bit rubbish, my navigator and I weren't quite in the flow, the weather was bad, our comms were a bit off, we missed a few targets and landed at Lossiemouth in Scotland to be told we'd failed the trip. My shoulders, still tense from the scrappy flight, now felt like someone had tied a knot in them.

I couldn't meet anyone's eyes as I awaited the summons for a quiet word. I felt like a dead woman walking.

The memories of those days were swirling around my head as I sat on the toilet in the bowels of St Hugh's in Oxford. I tried to turn the other cheek, so to speak, and started talking to myself, Right, Mands, let's look at the evidence. Has anyone actually said anything negative? Where is the evidence that these officers are looking down on you? It's your own negative thoughts that are swamping your brain, no one else's, so you have the power to make them go away. I again pictured positive receptions I'd had at speeches and thought about some complimentary emails I'd received and how they made me feel.

Since Vienna, I had developed a new technique, too. To encourage those positive vibes, I would flood my mind with a colour, in my case purple, to instill a sense of wellbeing. It seemed to force the chimp to slink away and go back to wherever it is she hides the rest of the time. It seems to help to recalibrate my mojo, allowing me to get on with being my best self.

"Tonight, Matthew..."

I emerged from the cubicle fortified and swathed in a metaphorical cloak of confidence. Well, a scarf or perhaps a small shawl of confidence, anyway. I strode back to the bar, allowing myself a small grin at my own little secret.

"What are you smiling at?" asked Craig.

"Nothing."

I'm not claiming to have transformed into a superhero, but I had at least succeeded in stopping the room spinning. Like in Vienna, I had been close to bringing about my own downfall, creating a scenario in my head and allowing it to play out. Like in Lossiemouth, the truth was somewhat different to my imagined reality. There, no one was preparing to tap me on the shoulder and show me the door.

I was told to brush up on a few bits, get back into the air, nail the trip and get ready to fly back to the Gulf. In Oxford, I'd come close to panicking, but I recognised what was happening and managed to do a decent morale-boosting job on myself, almost as if I was mentoring someone else.

This tale is the essence of controlling the controllables. I couldn't affect the thoughts or the actions of the senior officers, only how I presented myself and managed my own thoughts and emotions. As it turned out, the speech went well, as deep down I knew it would, to a bunch of boozed-up university cadets. None of the senior officers gave the slightest hint they thought I shouldn't have been there.

They were all very charming and complimentary.

This little blip is not something that I would have chosen to have gone through, but it did add another layer of experience, like a fresh coating of snow, which when it melts tops up the pool of resilience. This feeling of being out of your comfort zone, or that you're about to be found out as not quite good enough, is probably familiar to us all in some way, which in itself should tell you that it's a normal part of the process. Knowing that you're not alone – maybe there are others in that meeting who were feeling the same thing – could help you reframe what you're experiencing as nothing personal or a slight on you, but part of the territory, as normal as putting on socks. The further you can extend that comfort zone, knowing it could be a bit bumpy for a while but that's OK, the more space you'll have to grow.

But we're all human and sometimes we don't manage to focus on what we can control. We let emotion and imagination take over as it did with me that night in Oxford. We all like to think we don't care what others think of us, but let's be honest, most of us do. I certainly did.

And for a while, it held me back. It almost stopped me from making some of the best decisions of my life.

The first time I felt this acutely was after I left the military. I wanted adventure, I wanted a challenge and I wanted to prove to myself that I was still capable of handling the unknown. So, I bought a caravan and planned to take it to France for six weeks with my two young sons, aged seven and eight. Craig was working for most of the period so I would be flying solo.

But the moment I told people about my plan; the reaction was almost universal.

"Are you crazy?"

"That's way too big to do on your own."

"What if something goes wrong?"

At first, I was confident in my decision. But the more I heard the worries of others, the more I started to question myself. What if they were right? What if I really couldn't do it? What if I got stranded somewhere, unable to manage? Doubt was flooding my body like poison. I began to have sleepless nights turning over every possible disaster scenario in my head.

I went from feeling excited about the trip to feeling paralysed by fear.

It was ridiculous, really, because nothing had changed. My ability to tow the caravan hadn't disappeared overnight. The roads in France weren't suddenly more dangerous. The only thing that had shifted was the way I saw myself, because I'd let other people's voices replace my own.

I was still determined to go so I prepared properly, planning the routes, practising towing the caravan and working out contingency plans. Once we were on our glorious adventure, I solved challenges as they arose and above all, I trusted myself. I'd flown jets at 500mph, surely, I could handle a caravan at 50mph. We had an amazing time, but I realised how close I had come to letting fear steal that from me.

When I first started motivational speaking, I was embarrassed to post about it on social media. What if my friends thought I was arrogant? What if they thought I was getting too big for my boots? That fear kept me away from social media for years. But through conversations with others in business, I realised social media was one of my main platforms for growing my brand – essential to secure future speaking slots. I could either let my fear of judgment keep me small, or I could stop worrying about what people thought and just post anyway, which is what I did.

It's essential.

Often there is nothing to act as a brake on these negative emotions and they build like a snowball rolling down a hill. But occasionally there is real jeopardy involved, when controlling the controllables becomes far more significant. On September 11, 2001, I was flying my Tornado back to the UK after taking part in Red Flag, a two-week, multi-national air combat training exercise at Nellis Air Force Base, Las Vegas. We were a four-ship – four jets flying in formation behind a Tristar tanker for mid-air refuelling.

We'd broken the journey at Lajes on the Azores islands, nearly 1,000 miles into the Atlantic west of Portugal and had the final leg back up to Blighty to go. Chatting to the others on the radio that morning after taking off from Lajes, I was happy, life was good. But then the Tristar crew came on the radio to say their high-frequency unit was picking up some reports that American airspace had been locked down. They had no more information, but it meant that any aircraft heading west across the Atlantic bound for the US would be turning around.

The sky was about to become busy. Trouble was, by now we were flying in thick clouds and I couldn't see our formation outside our cockpit. The mystery and the lack of information immediately ignited the imagination, and we swapped a few brief comments over the radio, wondering what was going on. But we knew we had a more important task on our hands.

We flew on through the milky soup on instruments, scanning the radar to stay in touch with the formation and avoid any collisions. Our job was not to speculate, it was to get home safely. We had to treat this now like a high-stakes mission, controlling what we could and letting everything else go. Nothing mattered now but what we were doing in the confines of our cramped, metal cockpits.

Emotions went out of the window, figuratively rather than literally, as we focused on the screens, gauges and switches in front of us, ears pricked for any radio instruction. It was only after we landed back at RAF Marham that we learned of the full horror of the 9/11 attacks. In our situation, knowing the big picture wouldn't have helped us. We couldn't control that; we could only control ourselves.

So, the next time you find yourself stressing over opinions, outcomes or situations beyond your reach, ask yourself: is this something I can control? If the answer is no, let it go. It's a great way to reclaim your focus, peace and power.

CRAIG: It's illogical for me to get imposter syndrome. I've been flying for forty-five years and training pilots for quite a lot of that time, so how can I feel inadequate or not cut out for the job? But I do feel it sometimes, especially when it comes around to my yearly simulator test to make sure I'm still up to scratch. I've concluded that imposter syndrome is normal and it's OK as long as it doesn't limit you. In a way it fires me up and prevents me from being complacent.

In my world, if you don't get it right there can be serious consequences. You can't be flying around the sky half-heartedly; you must be at the right standard. Imposter syndrome is there; it just needs to be managed. You have to be dynamic about it.

I don't want to fail; I don't want to be publicly held up as not good enough in my job and clearly I don't want to fall short of safety standards. In part, it goes back to those school days and feelings of worthlessness.

To counter that, and to overcome the fear of failure in the first place which might prevent me from moving forward along my path, my coping mechanism is preparation. I will always be ultra-prepared, whether it is for a check ride, a course or a new role. I don't want to look like a fool. If there are some points to tidy up, and hopefully there are, because it's about developmental feedback, I'll accept them constructively.

But if I hadn't prepared and then I failed, I'd find that even more difficult to deal with because it would be my fault. Some people – like Mandy – are far happier to bound through life with the 'blag it' or 'wing it' mentality, preferring the 'fake it until you make it' approach. A lot depends on where you are on the introvert/extrovert scale. I'm an introvert by nature and am all about quiet determination and preparation, rather than taking a flying leap at the comfort zone to see how far I can get.

I certainly wouldn't have taken the Atomic Energy gig like Mandy did.

Initially, my prospects seemed bleak. It felt like every time I put my foot on the bottom rung of a ladder it broke and sent me crashing back down. I couldn't see how I was ever going to get off the ground. After failing the AIB I moped around for a few days, but I couldn't shake the feeling that my reasons for wanting to join the navy hadn't changed.

The motivation for a life of flying, adventure, camaraderie, travel and serving my country was still there. I began to realise that my failure to join the navy had actually stoked something inside. It had given me purpose. You can either give up and say that's the end of the road for me or you can find another angle.

My Dad suggested I write to the AIB for some feedback, so I carefully crafted my note and a week or so later I got an amazing letter back. They said I had shown good motivation and my leadership was strong, but they were just a bit worried about my academic side. They said being an officer in the Royal Navy was demanding and they were concerned about my ability to cope with the level of work. But they said I was welcome to go back in a year's time and try again.

Sometimes it's hard to hear the truth, but it was the inspiration I needed. Plus, my only other option was going back to work full time at Pirelli's.

"Can I put in an order for two metres of cable please..."

Now that I had lasered-on to the idea of joining the navy I was all in. Academics for the sake of passing exams didn't interest me, but now I was a man on a mission. Having been through the AIB once, and fuelled by the navy's encouraging letter, I didn't feel like an imposter anymore, or that I was hopelessly out of my depth. I felt it was within reach if I could just stretch a little bit higher.

I signed up for night school and studied for maths, physics and English O'level refreshers, working a nine to five at Pirellis before getting my head in the books for a few hours. I also thought I needed to show a bit of initiative, so I got involved in running a local football team. And I planned a big expedition to walk the 270 miles of the Pennine Way with my brother Paul. One day down the pub chatting about life, Paul decided he would have a crack at the navy too.

So being a bright boy, he went off and did physics O'level, as an additional exam, sat his AIB quickly and passed first time.

My board was still some way off and I practised writing the types of essays I knew would come up. I knew the final question they would ask me in the main interview would be whether there was anything else I would like to say, so I worked on this meticulously and prepared a speech which I memorised and practised to make it sound like I wasn't just repeating a script.

"You'll be aware I've been before the board before," I began, "and it was feared I would struggle academically. I agree I am no academic and although I have made big strides in this area, I hope and believe you're looking for more than that. I hope I've demonstrated my determination, motivation and commitment to join the Royal Navy and I believe I have other qualities you're looking for. I just ask you to give me a chance..."

On the day, it came out perfectly and I let my last line hang in the air, like smoke from a cannon drifting gently in the breeze. I looked with sincerity into the eyes of each panel member in turn. They thanked me for my time – shaking slightly I rose and headed to the door, trying not to trip on the way out. You've fired all your shots now, matey.

Nothing more you can do. Later that afternoon, I was called back to the interview room. The atmosphere felt different, less oppressive. Or was I just all out of ammo and resigned to my fate.

Hang on, is he smiling?

"Congratulations, Craig. You've passed the Admiralty Interview Board, and we recommend you join the Royal Navy as a pilot."

Britannia Royal Naval College in Dartmouth is a grand old red brick building on the green hills above the River Dart in south Devon. New officers have been trained there since 1905 and in the summer of 1984, it was home to two Hickson brothers. I went down to Dartmouth massively excited but also aware of my limitations. I told myself to embrace it for what it was, tackle what was in front of me and not worry too much about the what ifs further down the line.

I'd been burned too many times to get carried away. They're bound to see through you at some stage, matey, so just take each day as it comes and do your best.

The early weeks were like being strapped to a runaway train, eighteen hours a day of physical fitness, marching, cleaning and polishing kit, all on very little sleep. It was designed to stress you to see what you were really made of and build you back up to navy standards. At first, I was in awe of the college and everyone there. A couple of guys in my intake instantly stood out which didn't particularly help the self-esteem – one guy became the First Sea Lord and the head of the Royal Navy. He was a brilliant guy, charming, with a brain the size of the West Country and clearly destined for the top. Another guy became an admiral, was knighted and ended up as commander of NATO's Allied Maritime Command. He was also outstanding, although we all gasped in horror one day when he was seen wandering towards a spinning helicopter tail rotor blade, quite oblivious. Luckily, he was caught in time.

In the quieter moments, when the fatigue was really gnawing at the inside of my head, I questioned whether I was really up to scratch alongside these guys, in this venerable institution. But as another week passed without having been chucked out, I began to feel more confident in my sense of self. I realised that everyone was actually pretty similar, with strengths and weaknesses and plenty of inherent daftness. I could handle the physical side of it, that was just a case of sticking your head down and gritting it out.

And I enjoyed any exercises where we got a chance to lead the group. It felt quite natural and the others seemed to respond well to me which was a good boost. I realised I was enjoying being in the mix with everyone else and I felt like I belonged. There was clearly some merit to me being there otherwise I would have been kicked out by now, I reasoned.

Everyone had areas they struggled in and recognising this helped dispel some of the nagging thoughts of being an imposter in this world.

Unsurprisingly, the only area where I was on the back foot was in the classroom. At the end of the first term there were ten exams, including navy-specific subjects such as seamanship and navigation. If you failed three you could do them again but fail four and you were out. I failed three and scraped through Royal Navy history right on the pass mark of seventy.

I was as close as it gets to being chucked out, barring the shouting. The only reason I even did that well was because someone gave me some top tips as to what was on a previous exam paper. I re-sat the failed exams and squeezed out passes. I was clinging on by the skin of my teeth.

In the second term we got our first taste of flying down at Plymouth Airport, learning the rudiments in the two-seater Chipmunk training aircraft. This was my first flight in any airplane that I had control of. I loved everything about it, the controls, the kit, the views, the speed, the smell of aviation fuel. The Chipmunk was great fun to fly but a handful on the ground, a taildragger which means the nose is in the air and it's hard to see what you're doing.

One guy, a Canadian, would zig-zag down the taxiway virtually doing 360s. He didn't seem to be doing what the rest of us had been taught so we could only assume he was either doing the advanced course, or he had a crazy instructor.

Very quickly I contracted a severe case of the flying bug and I knew this was exactly what I wanted to do with my life. I was determined to give it everything. My brother Paul was on the course ahead of me and had managed to get chopped at the first hurdle. Unlike me, the night before his test he went out and got royally drunk, whereas I stayed in and studied.

He only really joined the navy because I did, his heart was not really in it. He had so many options still open to him, being younger and naturally academic. This for me was the real deal, my one chance to do something truly worthwhile.

I hung on despite the academics and managed to pass out from Dartmouth at the end of the thirty-week course. On a blustery day on the parade ground in front of the imposing old college I marched past my proud parents. Even that wasn't quite perfect, mind you, as my hat blew off while we were marching. So there I was, in the shop window, in full view of senior officers and a large contingent of family and friends, and I was negative of hat.

One of the staff retrieved it and deposited it back on my head as I was standing at attention. He leaned in close to my ear as he straightened it.

"Keep your bloody hat on, will you, sir."

So far, so good, but Dartmouth was only the first hurdle. I moved from there to Joint Elementary Flying Training (JEFTS) at RAF Linton-on-Ouse in Yorkshire. All aspiring pilots from the RN and RAF began their careers as aviators here. On the long drive up north, I kept catching myself thinking, I'm about to start flying training in the British military.

How cool is this? I almost had to stop myself telling everyone I met on the way up, from petrol station attendants to the lady selling me a sandwich in the motorway services.

"Hi, yeah, thanks... by the way I'm actually a pilot in the Royal Navy."

I wasn't yet, not by a long way.

We began our flying in Bulldogs and also took courses on aviation medicine, how the body copes with altitude, visual illusions and survival. I found I could cope okay with the hand-eye coordination needed for flying and I was getting more and more into it, loving that I was developing a skill that would hopefully become my proper career, because let's face it up until now the prospects for one of those had not been looking good. Even the more difficult stuff like the quick mental arithmetic needed for navigation wasn't totally beyond me – tough and stressful, but not so I was floundering. Where I was scrambling to keep up was the rote learning parts, such as understanding electrical systems out of a book.

While I had an idea of how I was getting on personally, it was hard to tell where I slotted into the hierarchy. There was one young, cocky guy called Charlie, who was great fun and had an arrogant swagger to him. In the crew room after a flight, I'd ask him how he got on.

"Yep, all good, no problem, I've got this," he'd reply, chomping on his gum as usual.

While I was doing okay, I knew I was near the edge of my envelope so I assumed Charlie must be acing it. One day I bumped into him coming out of the boss' office and I asked how his flight had been.

"Yep, all good, just been chopped," he said, chewing furiously.

Blimey, if Charlie's been chopped what hope have I got? It just shows you never know what's going on with other people, so it's best to keep out of your own way and not psyche yourself out by comparing yourself to others. That's a sure-fire way to let imposter syndrome take hold. That meeting you're in at work where you're feeling uncomfortable or out of your depth? Chances are you won't be alone.

JEFTS was tough but I relished the environment created by the two chief instructors, Arfur Bryant and Ray Harper. They had both served in the Falklands and seen plenty of action, but they didn't act the hero at all – they weren't trying to catch me out, they were just trying to get the best out of me. I tend to respond well to that method of learning and I gave it my all. Fortunately, I passed the course and was sent back to the navy to begin helicopter flying training on the Gazelle with 705 Squadron at RNAS Culdrose on the far south-west tip of Cornwall.

The Gazelle is a small single-engine helicopter, a bit like a sports car, nippy and manoeuvrable but lively and twitchy. I discovered this the first time I climbed in with my instructor and attempted to lift it into a hover a few feet above the ground. Mirroring my instructor, who had just given me a perfect demonstration fifteen feet into the Cornish sky, I positioned my feet on the rudder pedals, my right hand gently cradled the cyclic, the stick that effectively moves the aircraft forward, and with my left hand I clutched the collective, the control positioned like the hand brake on a car, that alters the pitch of the rotor blades to effect lift. I applied some left rudder to keep the aircraft straight and pulled on the collective to lift us into the air.

Only I had yet to learn the required levels of finesse and my graceless yank sent us soaring into the air like a jack-in-the-box. Trying to recover I eased off the collective and we plunged quickly towards the ground. Blimey, this is hard, how do they fly these things? Edging nearer to panic mode, I hauled on the collective again and up we spurted. I repeated this up and down a few more times, before finally settling back down on the turf, like a ball at the end of its bounce.

"Are you always this ham-fisted, Hickson?"

I gathered myself and tried again, this time easing up the collective in tiny increments until the Gazelle shook itself free of the ground and I was able to keep it at more or less a continuous hover. Looking forward and then to the side I used fixed references outside the cockpit to help stay in more or less the same position. Well, this is very cool. I'm hovering several tonnes of screaming metal in the air just by pulling a few levers.

From the hover I learned how to transition to forward flight by pushing the cyclic gently forwards to gain translational lift and then combine that with some collective to climb higher. There's lots more coordination involved than flying a fixed-wing aircraft and it uses all your hands and legs. Eventually I got to grips with the basics, but I did find instrument flying quite a head-scrambler and eventually failed a key trip. You could fail two and re-take them but fail a third, known as the air warning, and you were out.

Every successful flight and each course passed gave me a little bit more confidence, but I still felt like I was in a lift stuck between two floors, somewhere between success and failure.

From the Gazelle I graduated to the twin-engine Sea King Mark V helicopter, which would be my office for the next few years of operational flying. It could be armed with torpedoes, depth charges and a machine gun, and was crewed by two pilots, an observer and an aircrewman, who operated the sonar and the winch. Compared with the Gazelle it was a much more powerful aircraft, big and stable, with much larger instruments and it threw out a fairly violent 40 knot downwash, making life pretty uncomfortable for anyone directly below.

We began with lots of general handling, instrument flying and formation practice before learning how to fight the aircraft, using its weapons in its primary anti-submarine role and undertaking more advanced exercises with ships. Going back to the beginning with a new aircraft was refreshing but we were made well aware we weren't untouchable. I knew I had to knuckle down to get through each little stage. Of the twenty who started the course, only about ten qualified.

Was it necessary to chop everyone? I've got different feelings about it now, but that's how it was then.

Once up to speed I joined 826 Squadron, also at Culdrose, and immediately sensed a change in the atmosphere. Being an operational squadron, it was a much more adult approach and us junior joes were treated like human beings rather than just morons lucky to be there, as it had felt up until then. It was still the Cold War era and our main role was anti-submarine warfare, hunting down Russian subs and supporting our subs and surface ships. Soon I was posted out to a Royal Fleet Auxiliary (RFA) tanker called RFA Olmeda to spend some time up near the Arctic circle, listening, gathering information and protecting Royal Navy assets in the region.

One time, we'd been operating up near the Russian port of Murmansk for a couple of months, watching what was coming out of the port and letting them know we were there and keeping a general eye on things. Being the smart young aviators, we thought we were, we decided it would be a good idea to enhance international relations. Another Sea King crew packaged up a bag of goodies containing chocolate, sweets and reading material for men who spend too much time on their own. They dropped it over a Russian submarine resting on the surface.

The Russian crew grabbed the bag and waved. Our boys waved back and it was all very jolly. The gift was quickly taken down inside the sub. The Sea King returned to Olmeda and the crew were very pleased with themselves.

We all thought it was a great wheeze, until half an hour later signals reached the ship at the highest level of priority, wanting to know why and how we had sparked a huge diplomatic incident. We'd been accused of dropping items on sovereign Russian territory which could have far-reaching consequences. What we had dreamed up in the bar, thinking it would be a laugh and a good 'dit' to tell back home, was suddenly sparking diplomatic uproar, with messages presumably flying from the sub to Moscow, back to the UK and apparently right to the top and Prime Minister herself, Margaret Thatcher. The atmosphere onboard that night was charged.

The boss was spitting feathers.

"What the bloody hell did you idiots think you were doing? You're in the shit; I'm in the shit and it's going to take me hours to sort out this mess."

To his enduring credit, he smoothed it all over and eventually saw the funny side. It's not as if we were transferring nuclear codes, after all.

After a couple of years with 826 Squadron, I moved to 814 Squadron, still flying out of Culdrose but part of the air group attached to HMS Invincible, one of the navy's three aircraft carriers alongside HMS Ark Royal and HMS Illustrious. I had about a thousand flying hours by this stage and qualified as aircraft commander, meaning I now flew as the captain on my Sea King. As a second tourist I was deemed 'competent and experienced'. I was now required to be a mentor for the young pilots fresh out of flying training.

I also held the role of a division officer, looking after the welfare, support, career progression and disciplinary matters of about ten young sailors. Our duties ranged from family days, flying displays and casualty evacuations to joining HMS Invincible when she went to sea. We took part in exercises with the RAF or with the US Navy or other NATO partners, in the Atlantic or up near Norway for Exercise Cold Winter to work with the submarines in the shallow waters of the fjords and test the operational readiness of NATO's northern flank. We would have at least two Sea Kings airborne throughout an exercise, which takes a big effort in terms of the number of aircraft, crew and maintenance staff needed.

We would fly for four hours, debrief, eat, sleep for four hours, then back into the air and repeat. As part of the carrier group, we were literally at the sharp end of UK defence and the projection of naval air power. Sometimes we were involved in search and rescue, such as the time we had to locate a downed Harrier pilot who crashed just after take-off. Sadly, he lost his life in the incident.

Living on board the carrier, there was a real sense of esprit de corps among the squadrons. There were the aircrew from 849 Squadron who were specialists in airborne early warning and then there were the fast-jet pilots from 800 Squadron. Everyone was fiercely loyal to their own squadron, like fans with their local football teams, and when the bar was packed it would be pretty boisterous. Our squadron was housed on 2 Deck on Invincible and it was close-knit stuff, three to a cabin, with no real privacy.

You really had to get on with your 'oppos' as your mates are called in the navy. For four months in 1989 we toured the east coast of the US, combining some operational training, notably on the live ranges around Andros Island in the Bahamas, with liaison and international relationship-building duties. Otherwise known as cocktail parties. On HMS Invincible they invariably took place in the main hangar or sometimes on the open deck if the weather was right.

Guests would walk up the gangplank to be greeted by the captain and then filtered down towards little pockets of waiting officers. If your squadron oppos happened to be on escort duties, you might get introduced to some funny, interesting people or they might stitch you up with a glint in their eye and deliver some individuals with less potential. It was all very convivial and the drinks flowed. Once, I thought I was being a gracious and considerate naval officer by going to help out one of my oppos who had got stuck on his own with a rather fierce-looking, dour individual.

I glided into their space, all smiles and charm, but before I could get to the C of "My name's Craig..." my oppo had thinned out. Sneaking an anxious glance to my left to see if any help was at hand, another group of my so-called mates all raised their glasses in my direction with wide grins on their faces before resuming their chats. My heart sank. I was now stuck and needed to summon all my new-found small talk skills to effect a soft landing and escape with all parties unscathed.

Towards the end of my time on 814 Squadron a communication came around saying the navy was looking for decent pilots with some experience to convert to the Sea Harrier, the single-seat vertical take-off and landing fighter jet. The pinnacle. I'd always wanted to go fixed-wing at some point so I put my name forward. My end of tour assessment read: 'A talented officer with above average flying ability. He has fully justified selection for Sea Harrier training.' Not bad for the lad who was told to never again darken the doors of that school. It just goes to show that despite its initial reservations, the Royal Navy really was after well-rounded individuals, not just academic whizz-kids. Your difference is your superpower they say, and it's clear I had plenty to offer outside the traditional learning environment. Perhaps the book worms weren't quite so effective at cocktail parties.

So, remember that there is more than one way in life. Potential lies in all of us; it's just that for some people it takes a bit longer to find.

Your path is your path.

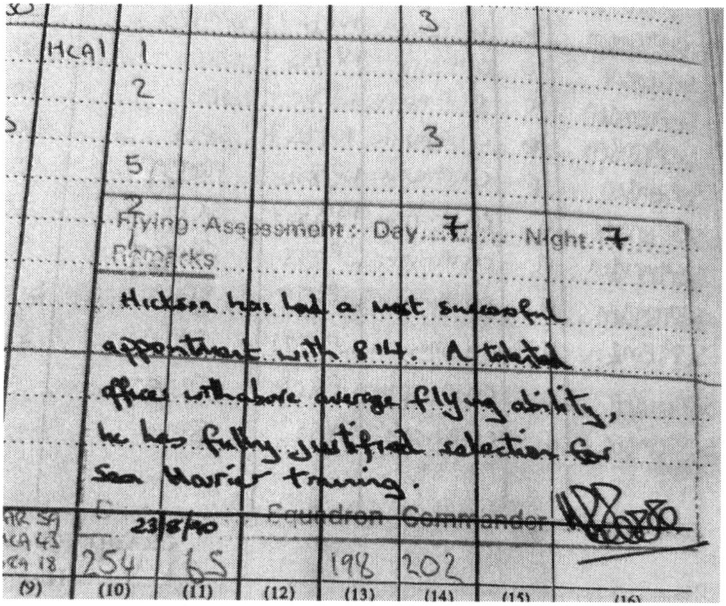

CHAPTER 4

LEVELLING OUT

MANDY: I just couldn't get my head around those stupid turns. Panic was closing in on me like the tide advancing on someone stuck in quicksand. I needed to master battle turns to be able to pass my fast jet course and get my wings to move on to the Tornado at RAF Valley, but time was running out. My brain fogged up every time I tried to even visualise what was required of me.

Battle turns are all about knowing when to make a turn so that you maintain position with your wingman when flying in formation. Flying a Hawk at 420 knots, it requires a grasp of the big picture and a few quick mental calculations to end up in the right place, but I just couldn't picture what I was trying to achieve. As the final check flight loomed, I spent the evenings locked in my room waving model airplanes around trying to figure out the positioning and the geometry to make the turns work. My virtual stress bucket was overflowing and leaving a nasty stain on the carpet.

Mandy, why can't you do this? It was only when my course mates took me onto the parade ground one night and demonstrated the manoeuvres on their bikes that the penny dropped. I passed, but it was close and I'd struggled through some soul-searching lows to get there.

While that was a remarkable display of team spirit from my peers, it was the culture set by the squadron boss which laid the foundations. Months earlier I had asked if I could leave my accommodation on the base and rent a little place on my own. As the only female on the course, I felt I needed some space. I thought it was a reasonable, grown-up request but the boss flatly refused.

He insisted we all needed to live together on the base, going through the same experiences. This would foster a deep-rooted affinity with each other, he said. I was unconvinced and felt hard done by, a computer-says-no decision with little empathy for modern people. Cycling around that parade ground by torchlight, with the fog clearing and battle turns beginning to make sense, I realised how wrong I was.

The boss's decision was all about creating the right environment for the team to function effectively. Yes, we were all individuals trying to get through a course, but one person's weakness didn't make the rest stronger and give them a better chance of passing. We were better as a collective, helping each other, relying on each other, like we might have to do if we ever had to fly actual combat missions against an angry enemy.

My first flying instructor at the university air squadron was very much from the old school. He ruled by fear and used to terrify most students. Some of his methods just wouldn't be acceptable today, not that they were then, but like much from that time he seemed to get away with it. At the start of one trip with him as we taxied out to the runway, I had to show that I had learnt all the 'mouth music', or correct terminology, for my pre-take-off instrument checks.

I really had learned it, up to a point anyway, although Wednesday afternoon netball followed by a session in the pub had slightly got in the way. Whatever, when I squeezed the rudder to the left, I was supposed to say:.

"Turning left, needle left, ball right, numbers decreasing and decreasing."

Then I kicked the rudder pedals the other way and was supposed to say:

"Turning right, needle right, ball left, numbers increasing and increasing."

I knew exactly what I needed to say except I just couldn't get the words out properly, in anything like the right order. I floundered on with some gibberish before he slammed the brakes on, fixed me with a stare:

"It's not bloody difficult, if you can't get it right, I won't fly with you again."

Part of me felt like a six-year-old, admonished for spilling my drink over the table again. Some of me was a little bit amused at his tantrum. The rest of me was furious. What kind of instruction is this? I'm trying, I'm just messing it up a bit.

A short while later, when he had got over himself, I was up flying with him again and supposed to be demonstrating how to keep the aircraft straight and level. But it was a bit out of balance, meaning I wasn't applying enough rudder to straighten it out. I was staring out through the front canopy, shoulders knotted and eyes fixated on the horizon. I hoped I was doing a good enough job not to get found out, but I was aware it wasn't perfect.

Suddenly, I felt a burning sensation in my left thigh. I yelped, thinking I'd been stung by a bee, but I looked down to see his fist clenched around the handle of his flying knife making a deep imprint in the dark green material of my flying suit.

Looking straight ahead he said: "I just wanted to check you had some life in your leg as you don't seem to be using it for the rudder."

He hadn't actually pierced my skin, but he was gently stabbing it with the tip of his knife, normally reserved for emergencies such as cutting your way out of a parachute. It was certainly at the more caveman end of the instruction spectrum and not an ideal way to get the best out of someone. It's a bit like the old stories of swimming teachers chucking kids into the deep end and making them figure it out. Yes, it probably gets a result in the end but what a terrible way to go about it.

In both cases, the environment he created was less than ideal and, to me at least, the wrong way to get results.

Contrast that with the head instructor at RAF Valley when I was struggling in fast jet training. I had messed up a couple of navigation tests from being just not quite sharp enough with my thoughts and actions. I faced a final check flight, which could possibly be make or break depending on how badly I did. As each day of this section of training wore on, I was feeling more exposed and under the spotlight, as if my every move was being examined and critiqued, even out of the jet.

My confidence was shaking, like a weightlifter's legs. I sensed I was about to buckle and send everything I'd worked for crashing to the ground. On the day of the flight, the chief instructor, Wing Commander Ray Lock, greeted me with a big smile and some friendly chit-chat before laying out the parameters of the mission. He pointed out a couple of places on the map that I might want to pay attention to and we set off.

His voice and words had set the tone, and as I went through my pre-flight checks in the cockpit, I felt calm and in control. I can do this. This is what I do. Rather than being under the microscope I felt like I was there to show off my skills, proud of what I could do, like a gardener showing off their prize courgette at the village show.

The flight went without a hitch and back in the debrief over a cup of tea I asked the instructor why he had gone easy on me. He hadn't, he replied, standards have to be met. But he had looked over my record and realised it wasn't a flying issue I was having; it was a confidence issue. By creating the right environment, he had given me the platform to perform.

It would have been easy for him to go in hard, play the bad cop throughout and boast to his colleagues back in the mess how he weeded out the lone female in the intake. But his approach was a perfect example of an enlightened and empowering leader and a lesson I will never forget. As pivotal moments go in my career, this was right up there.

The environment in which we work has a large bearing on our happiness and effectiveness. We all know that from our own negative experiences, perhaps of an unreasonable boss, a toxic colleague or less than satisfactory working conditions. At some point on your path, you may find yourself in a position of influence and you owe it to your colleagues to create the right environment in which they can give their best. You might not have any say in the colour of the carpet or the hardness of the chairs, but you can affect the environment through your interaction, communication, empathy and motivation.

It's part of being an effective leader.

As an individual there are some things you can't control,

and clearly one person's hellish environment might be another's idea of heaven. Whatever your environment, it is up to you to choose how you react to it. You can embrace it, try to adapt to it, try to change it, or decide it is not for you and look to move on. One hurdle I had to overcome in my RAF days was a lack of women-specific long johns to wear under flying kit.

It might sound like a small thing but throughout my career I sported fetching men's long johns with the Y-front fly and no allowances for a woman's curves. Great, eh?

I could have chosen to be offended and cause a storm when I found my room wallpapered with pornography every time I went on a combat tour to the Gulf. Instead, I answered it with humour, stripping it off the walls and throwing it out into the corridor with a cry of "Porn's up, boys". Sometimes others can be useful allies, like the team-mates at RAF Valley who called out the casual sexism from the instructors as they made comments about how I had parked my jet or whether I had put on my lipstick. None of the individual instructors were deliberately creating a poor environment for me but my classmates saw the bigger picture.

They surmised that all these comments combined could eventually take their toll on me and they took their misgivings to the boss. The fact I was oblivious, or had chosen to ignore it, is beside the point.

Even if you are not responsible for creating the environment at a macro level with company cultures or by shaping a large team, there is one environment we're all responsible for and that is the environment we create around ourselves. We all have it in our power to control how we project ourselves and interact individually with people. This is personal leadership. You owe it to your future path to make the environment around you a good one, radiating as far out as your sphere of influence extends.

Everyone around you will benefit, including you.

A few years ago, Craig and I signed up with a tour company for a fourteen day trip trekking to Everest Base Camp, an adventure we had been longing to do for ages. We flew out to Kathmandu, a whirling, deafening, dusty maelstrom of a city with the white-capped Himalayan peaks as a backdrop. The constant buzz of motorbikes and scooters gave the impression of millions of bees humming around a hive. In Thamel, the tourist quarter, the narrow, old streets and winding alleys are lined with mostly ramshackle brick shops selling all kinds of trekking and climbing gear, some of it even genuine.

There are myriad travel agencies and craft shops; here and there a bookshop stuffed full of well-worn paperbacks; and the tantalising waft of food from street stalls, cafes and restaurants, squeezed in between cheap hotels and guesthouses. The onset of dusk, with twinkling lights, every flavour of music and the drifting scent of a thousand incense sticks just increased the magic. In the bar of our hotel, we met the other members of the team we would be trekking with. There were a couple of expats living in Dubai, a lovely Scottish lady travelling on her own and six guys in their early 30s from Wigan, who were boisterous and full of energy.

They immediately began ordering pints of lager and I found myself joining in, accepting pints and exaggerating my Manchester accent, keen to match their northwest of England vibe. Looking back, it was reminiscent of my old traits from the RAF, trying to fit in and be one of the boys. Even at this stage of my life, with a successful speaking career, often espousing the virtues of being yourself, I was still vulnerable to changing like a chameleon to fit the environment I was in, rather than being strong and retaining my identity. Craig even gave me a look that said, "What are you doing?".

The following day we climbed into a small, beaten-up coach, with our gear piled on the roof and drove for six hours to the airport at Ramechhap east of Kathmandu. There we climbed into a tiny propeller plane for the thirty-minute hop up to Lukla, the infamous runway perched on the side of a deep valley at the entrance to Everest's Khumbu region. It's infamous because there have been a number of tragic accidents on take-off and landing up there. It's a bit like trying to land on a tea tray balanced on the side of the mountain.

From the town of Lukla at 2,800m we eased into the rhythm of the trek, walking with daypacks with a team of local porters carrying our main kit. Our head guide Bal warned us not to pass the lead porter, both to save our energy and make sure we acclimatised slowly. However, the Wigan lads saw everything as a physical challenge and steamed past, disappearing up the trail. Often, we didn't know where they were or if they had taken the right route, causing some angst and bad feeling among the team.

I kept thinking about a trek I'd done to the summit of Kilimanjaro, Africa's highest mountain, with a group of women. We had all steadfastly stuck to the rules concerning pacing and acclimatisation, trusting the guides' knowledge and experience. Though it was a serious physical and mental challenge which we all had to dig deep for at various moments, the majority of us managed to summit, thanks to the guidance offered. Now, these guys were already ignoring the rules and shattering the group harmony.

The rest of us walked at our own pace, chatting and getting to know each other or sometimes luxuriating in silence and our own space as we took in the stupendous scenery of rhododendron forests, snow-clad mountains, deep gorges and nerve-jangling rope or wire suspension bridges.

The Wigan boys were interesting to chat to as individuals and on the whole lovely guys. Craig had plenty of meaningful chats as he trudged up the trails with one of them, a tree surgeon who had always wanted to join the Army but hadn't managed to summon the courage of his convictions. Craig gave him plenty of practical advice and offered to write him a recommendation. But when they regrouped the pack mentality kicked in and they became boisterous and overpowering.

At mealtimes, belching became an Olympic sport while mornings were greeted by a competitive chorus of phlegm removal, snorting, nose clearing, spitting and coughing. In the tea houses, other groups would be quietly sipping tea, chatting or playing cards but our guys seemingly had little empathy for anyone else and became the centre of attention wherever we went. A lot of the banter was funny and to be taken with a pinch of salt, but it was non-stop, loud and often fairly uncouth, even for a couple of military pilots who have seen it all.

Over lunch on the third day, I spotted Aileen sitting quietly on her own and popped over for a chat. In a soft voice she said she was fed up. The lads were already getting on her nerves and she feared they would ruin her once-in-a-lifetime trip, the adventure she had dreamed of for years and saved hard for. She was no shrinking violet, she was a hardcore Scottish hill walker, but their constant high-energy presence was starting to wear her down.

I was inclined to agree with her. Trying to help, I remembered the mindset tool I'd recently read about in the book *High Performance* by Jake Humphrey and Damian Hughes. It is a simple equation: E + R = O. It stands for Event + Response = Outcome.

The idea is that we can't always control an event, but we can control our response to it and that determines the outcome. We clearly couldn't change the guys in any significant way, so our only real solution to the problem was to change our reaction. Rather than let it fester and build into a bigger trip-defining issue we had to find a way, in our own heads, to get around it.

I suggested one way might be to shift the focus from frustration to curiosity or even compassion. Instead of resisting their energy, we could try to reinterpret it, perhaps reframing the group not as an annoyance, but as a source of entertainment and camaraderie, something to observe rather than absorb. We resolved to get to know them as individuals, finding common ground with each one. That simple change in response transformed the experience.

There were still times when they infuriated us, but we felt more able to laugh along with them or take ourselves off for a quiet moment without resentment. The event hadn't changed. The people hadn't changed. But our response had and so did the outcome.

More or less. It was a great lesson that in any environment, we can choose how we react, whether that is the workplace or in our personal lives. We can't always shift the external noise, but we can choose how we internalise it. And that choice often defines whether we feel overwhelmed or in control.

CRAIG: SMAC 309 came with a dangerous reputation. The name itself sounds funky, like the call sign for some sort of covert, behind-the-lines mission, but it really stands for Short Miscellaneous Air Course. Whatever, it was the gateway to flying the Sea Harrier and was infamous for being tough, intense and hardcore. Most people who took it failed, although the navy didn't say you had failed, it said you were assessed as not being a suitable candidate.

To become a Harrier pilot and be acknowledged as having that level of competence and ability would be the pinnacle of a flying career and sit with you forever. I knew I would be moving up a couple of gears and it would be fast and furious, which appealed on the surface. However, the Sea Harrier was a very demanding aircraft to fly. Being a single seat, you had to fly it, operate a radar and manage the weaponry.

You were also mainly flying over the sea and it was vertical take-off and landing, primarily onto an often moving, heaving aircraft carrier. It was also very fast if you'd come from helicopters, jumping up to 450 knots compared with 90 knots for a Sea King. Things happen quickly at this speed and mental arithmetic, navigation and decisions need to be super sharp. The people flying Sea Harriers were a small, elite group, very much the navy's top guns of the day.

They carried themselves with a certain swagger. They were good and they knew it.

I left Culdrose and rocked up at RNAS Yeovilton in Somerset for three months of SMAC action. We wouldn't be flying Harriers at first, of course, the conversion was undertaken in the Hawker Hunter, one of the RAF's second-generation swept-wing combat jets which by my time was a two-seater trainer. All of a sudden, us helicopter pilots were moving at seven miles a minute which compared with the Sea King was like pulling straight onto the fast lane of the motorway after bimbling around the country lanes for hours. It meant all our reactions had to be razor sharp, both our thought processes and calculations and general alertness.

Fuel was suddenly a real issue too. In the Sea King I'd never had to worry too much about whether I had enough fuel but now I could only last for about forty-five minutes at low level, so my navigation needed to be spot on.

In terms of getting airborne, flying around a circuit and landing, I managed to hold my own and progressed to flying solo without an instructor. But the complexities then piled up like a layer cake as we moved on to instrument flying, navigation and formation flying. With each trip I could feel my stress building and I knew I wasn't reaching the required standard. To make matters worse, the environment created by the instructors was hard-nosed.

There was no nurturing, no support, no help. It was very much sink or swim, here's the jet, here's the check-list, get on with it. It was all about how you could cope. It turns out I wasn't coping very well.

I knew I thrived when I was supported, encouraged and praised. I'd learned the hard way at school that if you criticise or demean me, I quickly spiral downwards. But the instructors at SMAC 309 weren't there to praise, they were there to find out who could hack it. Once you get into that spiral descent mentally, it's very hard to pull out and that's when you crash and burn, hopefully not literally.

One of the instructors was okay but I just didn't feel comfortable with the main guy, I thought he was out to get me.

My reserves of confidence were quickly draining away, like air seeping out of a punctured tyre. And let's not forget, I was an experienced navy pilot at this stage, not some clown off the street, but he created a very toxic environment, in my view.

The trip which ended it for me was a low-level detail in which I was supposed to find and bomb a target, which turned out to be a cluster of deserted farm buildings in mid-Wales. I was struggling to get into the right position and even though I could see the target, I wasn't wings-level and ready to attack. Flipping heck, come on, man, what's the matter with you? Getting flustered, I decided to go around and have another shot and got a bit lost with my navigation. I had become fixated on the task and wasn't paying attention to my fuel, and at low level you burn through it much quicker.

Crikey, I'm really low on fuel. What a mess... better get back up to high level quick.

Craig, you twit.

The instructor was in the seat next to me watching my every move and he said he would take the controls for the trip home. I knew then I was done for. He called Yeovilton for a priority landing, but they said no, so we had to divert to RAF Chivenor as we didn't have enough fuel to wait for Yeovilton to clear and maintain our diversion fuel (a minimum fuel needed on landing). In a way he cocked up more than me because he was in charge and allowed me to get to this stage, but that's a moot point.

Finally, back at base I met him in his office and he was friendly enough, but it was bad news.

"I'm sorry Craig, I really hate doing this and remember, it's not a chop ride, you've done nothing wrong, but you are assessed as not being of a sufficient standard to recommend for further Harrier training."

In a way it was an utter relief. I knew I wasn't coping and I was sinking quickly. I could fly the airplane, but I just couldn't operate it at a high enough level. But it was disappointing too, my one chance to fly a Harrier gone.

It still sits with me now. On my course of four, one guy passed, one dropped out for medical reasons but was allowed to go back later and two of us didn't make it.

I found it hard to ignore the SMAC 309 environment, and I accept that. Some people did pass so I need to take responsibility for my own performance, behaviours and attitude. It's worth thinking about, though. If you're in a situation where the environment is not right for you, what are you going to do? Accept it for what it is and adapt? Try to hang in there but possibly against your instinct? Try to change the environment? Or roll over and say you can't hack it? There's nothing wrong with this last one, by the way, if it gets you out of a poisonous situation.

Often you might have to do a bit of all of them, and of course it depends on your motivation. Can you change your mindset enough or are you unwilling to compromise? But recognising you're in a less than perfect environment for you might just be the first step to doing something about it, whatever route you end up taking.

I have since flown a lot with Harrier pilots in various aircraft and most, but not all of them, are extraordinarily talented. One of the biggest differences I've noticed between the normal Joes and the fast jet jocks is the ability to move on. Everyone, and I mean everyone, makes mistakes in the air, but it's those pilots who can fix the problem and put it quickly behind them that prosper in that elite environment. I was dwelling on the mistakes, thinking, "Oh heck, this is it, they'll get me on this." It becomes a self-perpetuating problem and you lose the capacity to focus on the actual task.

But what about if we flip it and look at the SMAC 309 environment from a training point of view. Now you are a leader or an instructor or a coach, what type of environment are you going to create? To me in my pilot examiner role nowadays, the purpose of a trainer is to get the best out of the trainee, it's not to crucify them. Clearly, in our world of aviation you can't push people forward who aren't up to the required standard, that's crazy in anyone's book for obvious safety reasons. But you can create an environment in which people have a chance to perform at their best.

People have different learning styles and as an instructor I spend a lot of time trying to decipher how to get the best out of each student. Maybe the SMAC 309 guys were looking for that hardcore, best-of-the-best alpha mentality but I suspect they missed out on some very capable pilots because of it. I often wonder whether I would have passed the course if the environment was different? Honestly, probably not. Could I have done better and shown my true potential and abilities? Absolutely, yes.

What you learn when you change jobs every few years, such as in the military, is that as one door closes, others open and often lead you down paths you never dreamed of. When Harrier conversion didn't work out, I was sent to 772 Squadron, based at RNAS Portland, near Weymouth in Dorset on the south coast of England. One of its main functions was search and rescue (SAR) flying the Sea King Mark IV. It was an extraordinarily rewarding role and I thought at the time it was the best job I was ever going to have, which goes to show you never know what is around the corner.

There is nothing more satisfying than to be called out on a 'shout' to rescue someone and to save lives. We operated in a three-man crew, with a single pilot, a crewman who operated the winch, and a diver. We did a lot of rescues, about a third of which were stricken divers. Sadly, about a third of those lost their lives, often before we got there.

One day I was sitting around the crew room reading the paper when the piercing shrill of the klaxon on the wall shook me from my musings about the latest celebrity gossip.

I flung the paper down, leapt up and ran through the door to the helipad, pulling up my green goon suit as I went. The engineers were running out with me and it was our goal to get airborne in three minutes. I climbed into the cockpit, grabbed my helmet from its hook and stuffed it on my head, switched on the batteries and pushed the button to start the first engine. We'd already had a practice start when we first came on shift and had left the aircraft in a state of readiness, albeit without the engines running.

Strapping myself in I started the second engine and when that was lit the engineer standing in front of the glass bulb of the cockpit gave me the whirly hand signal to fire up the rotors. As the low, slow whine worked itself into a roaring fury, the diver and crewman jumped in, put their helmets on and connected the intercom so we could communicate.

"Head east," said Bilbo, my crewman.

This was all I needed for now and I pulled on the collective to lift the bird off the ground. For a ten-tonne monster she sprang lightly into action and soon we were up and away.

"Child, cliff fall, Lulworth Cove, transit time five minutes," said Bilbo, again all business. I could feel the blustery wind gusting as we made the short hop across Weymouth Bay to Lulworth Cove on the Dorset coast. It's a deep horseshoe-shaped cove with lovely blue water on a sunny day, backed by some steep cliffs, some covered in grass and some exposed rock. Flying over the headland I could see a coastguard vehicle on the cliff and a gaggle of people.

I flew in closer to see if we could get eyes on the casualty, which we'd heard by now was a young boy. Whisky, our diver, spotted something about 60 feet down the cliff. I tried to remain dispassionate, but it didn't sound good. As Whisky prepared his kit to get on the winch, Bilbo started to direct me in.

In a helicopter it's always better to hover into the wind because the air flowing under the rotors puts less strain on the engine and so gives a better performance. The trouble was, with this wind direction that meant edging in backwards to the cliff, keeping the open door on the aircraft's right to the rocks so we could lower Whisky. From my seat, I couldn't see the cliff at the back or the tips of the rotor blades twenty feet away, so I was effectively flying blind, totally reliant on my team to help me in.

"Back five, four, three, two, one, steady," said Bilbo as I just concentrated on flying the aircraft.

"Come right, five... steady."

To maintain your position when flying a helicopter, you have to use static visual references outside the cockpit, so I was focusing on a rock outcrop at the front and scanning for a feature to use out of my right window. But my gaze kept getting drawn by a woman standing right on the edge of the cliff with her hand on her head, jumping up and down and clearly very agitated. It dawned on me that this could be the mother of the boy and I was momentarily transfixed, my mind running through the emotions I would have felt if it was one of my children down there and I had no idea whether they were dead or alive. I jolted quickly out of this reverie and gave myself a talking to.

Craig, focus. Just fly the aircraft.

Whisky was now out of the helicopter and on his way down the cliff face on the winch. In those days there were no comms once he was outside, so he was talking to Bilbo through hand signals. I was just holding the ship steady in the gusts and focusing on my references as Whisky landed on the ledge where the boy was.

It was a thin, sloping sliver of rock, and we had to hope the 40-knot downwash from our rotor blades didn't blow the boy off before we could secure him. After a couple of minutes, Whisky looked up at Bilbo peering out of the helicopter and gave him a big thumbs up to say the boy seemed remarkably well. He placed his strop over the boy and Bilbo pressed the button to begin winding them back into the helicopter.

"Whisky has casualty in a double lift strop, winching now," he said to me as I was oblivious to what was going on back there.

"Five feet from door... casualty onboard, diver secure."

They laid the boy down and gave him a quick once over, but it did in fact seem as if he was unhurt. He must have landed like a cat, but he definitely lost one of his lives that day. Normally with a casualty we would go straight to hospital, but we had a quick chat on the radio with the coastguard on the cliff and we agreed it was best to reunite him with his mother. The coastguard also had a doctor in the team who could make a further assessment. I lifted out of the hover, pleased to be free of the need for such intense focus and surveyed a spot on the grassy cliff top to land.

When our wheels touched, Whisky jumped out and helped the boy off the helicopter. Pushing him into a crouch because of the downwash, they rushed over to the woman who was obviously his mum or guardian. The boy and the woman hugged as if they would never let go and I sat in the cockpit watching with tears filling my eyes. It was just a job, but at times like these it was far more than that. It was also the epitome of teamwork, every person and role vital in achieving a successful mission, none effective without the others.

Another key part of 772 Squadron was maritime counter terrorism (MCT), essentially part of the response force should any UK assets at sea be put at risk by aggressive actions.

When we were on this MCT rotation, we would be on standby to move in 12 hours. We were the unit to go in and sort out any trouble. And when I say sort it out, I mean properly sort it out. There would be three 'lifters' or Sea Kings carrying special forces soldiers, tooled up to the eyeballs, two Lynx helicopters acting as snipers, with guns to take out any 'baddies' on the way in, and a heavy-lift Chinook as back-up.

We spent a lot of time practising on ships in the English Channel or up in Scotland on the oil rigs. We'd fly at fifty feet over the sea in the dark wearing night vision goggles with no lights visible to alert the unsuspecting enemy. The snipers would go in about a minute ahead of us and then we would make our final approach, converting speed to height, by raising the nose and climbing up to establish on the target. The second we were stable the rope would be out of the side door of the helicopter and the first man would rapid-rope down it.

They were the ultimate professionals and didn't mess about and within about twenty seconds all of them were down the rope and onto the heaving, wet deck of the ship or rig. The instant I heard, "Last man down and rope secure" I would pull away as the next lifter would be coming straight in on my position. It was incredibly exhilarating flying, as good as it gets, and I would be buzzing for hours afterwards.

Working with the special forces, both SAS and SBS, was extremely rewarding as they're a different breed and have a real confidence about them. At the start of one training day we were meeting up on the airfield to brief the mission.

The special forces crew were sleeping in the hangar on the opposite side, but instead of driving around the perimeter road like they were supposed to, they just steamed straight across the grass and runway in their beat-up old Land Rovers. One of our senior officers started the briefing with a bit of light housekeeping, saying they weren't really allowed to do that as it was an active airfield and therefore dangerous, to which the special forces guys just shrugged and said, "So what?" I'm guessing their perception of risk was pretty different to ours.

But the real takeaway from working with the special forces and something I still use all the time now is the way they communicated, particularly in briefings. Everyone had a voice, from the youngest, most inexperienced new recruit up to the top person.

Once we'd briefed the weather, the target and the layout of the ship their boss would brief how they were going to get the ship back, whether that was attacking the bridge or the engine room or wherever. What I loved was that even the most junior member could pipe up and say, "Sir, that's a bad idea. If we do that, we'll get slotted in the head or ditched over the side…" If there was a dissenting voice, they'd all rethink it and maybe come up with a new plan. It was blunt and brutal but refreshing.

The point is that everyone had to be bought into the task, both to get the best possible outcome and to empower everyone in that team. It was a classic case of creating the right environment for everyone to give their best. No one would get shouted down or belittled, every voice was valued. The leaders still had overall authority but the whole team had a licence to provide input.

I've always remembered that and have tried to take it with me throughout my career.

At one of Mandy's recent gigs at the Pendulum Summit in Dublin, I tagged along to support her. Early one morning I hit the hotel gym and found myself alongside Ant Middleton, the former special forces operative, who was a guest speaker at the event. I couldn't resist breaking the ice, so I asked what he was doing there and introduced myself. As an SBS soldier he comes with a fearsome reputation, but I found him charming, interesting, willing to engage and talk military stuff.

We even managed to sink some of the black stuff together in the Ferryman Inn later that night. His performance on stage at the summit was full of energy but his message caught me by surprise. He talked about his own fear of failure and how you can't do it all on your own. He brought up a story from his second tour of duty in Afghanistan when he had struggled.

Apparently, he was tasked to lead a troop of four into a small compound and neutralise the threats. During the engagement he spotted a lone target disappearing into a smaller outhouse and knew they would need to deal with this. The target was hiding in a small room behind a closed door. Ant and his team took up positions outside the door and watched for a few moments.

They noticed that the enemy was spraying bullets at the door from the inside with his weapon in automatic mode, rather than in single-shot mode preferred by more professional soldiers to conserve ammunition. He would start at the bottom of the door and fire up until he reached the roof. Ant knew that when the bullets were at the top of the door it was his moment to engage and enter the building. But when the time came, he couldn't move.

He had frozen, he said.

At this point, one of his mates came up close behind him and just squeezed his shoulder. No words, nothing else, just a physical contact meaning they were there with him and they had his back. When the next rotation of bullets started flying towards the sky they entered and completed their task.

We all think these icons have it all, but often they don't; they are just like you and me. We all need help at some point. By creating that environment of trust, teamwork, camaraderie and honesty, Ant and his mates got the job done.

Even though I was loving 772 Squadron I had this itch I needed to scratch. I really wanted to become a QFI (qualified flying instructor) and I had been bugging my navy appointing officer to send me on the course. He kept replying that it wasn't the right time, that I needed more operational experience. Determined to find a way and to help support my case, I joined the team at 6AEF (Air Experience Flight) at RAF Benson in Oxfordshire, UK. This involved heading off in my spare time at the weekends to fly with air cadets aged from thirteen to eighteen years old.

I enjoyed the instructing and got a kick out of seeing the kids buzzing after their flights and progressing their skills.

I'd never forgotten those two heroes from JEFTS, Ray Harper and Arfur Bryant. They just exuded class, the way they talked to people, the way they cajoled their students, their status, aura, responsibility, knowledge. I wanted to be just like them. Forget fast jet flying, these guys were my real idols, quietly creating the right environment to get the best out of their students.

It wasn't about them trying to prove how tough they were as instructors; it was about making a positive difference to the people they were teaching.

Ray once failed me on a trip, when he simulated a failing engine. I had to fly a glide circuit and land a no-engine approach, but my speed was about five knots too slow. I was trying to eke it out, but I should have gone around and accepted I wasn't going to make it. It was late on a Friday afternoon and after failing I felt terrible for the rest of the weekend.

I bumped into Ray again much further down the line when we were both airline pilots and he admitted he should never have failed me because he recognised the adverse effect it would have on me. He knew I was a dweller on mistakes. He was right to fail me, of course, it was a safety issue, but he said getting to the root cause of why I was five knots slow and why I had failed to make the correct decision to go around might have been a more productive training technique.

I said a fond farewell to 772 Squadron and headed up to the now-defunct RAF Scampton in Lincolnshire, at that point home of the 'Dambusters', for three months of learning how to be a flying instructor and how to teach in the Bulldog, a workhorse of a trainer. Once I'd completed that I got to follow in the footsteps of my heroes and become an instructor at JEFTS out of RAF Linton and then RAF Cranwell, taking students through their elementary flying course. It was at this point I met a young RAF officer named Mandy Wells. I ended up marrying her.

After three years I was on the move again, and I managed to trade up my wheels from the Firefly to the Jetstream executive turboprop, training navigators out of Culdrose or based out of Royal Naval Air Station (RNAS) Yeovilton. As part of what was known as Heron Flight, we were also tasked with flying all ranks from the top brass to sailors, to destinations across Europe, including the areas of conflict of Northern Ireland and Bosnia. It was a good job, especially if you had aspirations to become an airline pilot. One day I bumped into an old colleague, Chris Greaves who was a few years ahead of me and always seemed to keep an eye out for me and my career.

He told me of a vacancy in his department at the Naval Flying Standards Flight which oversaw all the fixed-wing operations in the navy.

Aside from the Harrier, the navy operated a handful of other fixed-wing aircraft including the Jetstream, the

Chipmunk and the Hawk. We were a unit of three people, two Harrier guys and me. It was our job to assess the operational standards on each aircraft, which required us to learn all about them so we could offer knowledge and different perspectives. The Harrier guys had that one sewn up, but they were also keen to focus on the Jetstream, which meant there was a slot for me to learn how to fly the Hawk.

Absolute result. I couldn't believe my luck. I'd always stuck up my hand and jumped in the backseat of a Hawk whenever there had been a chance at various bases over the years, so I was very familiar with the airplane.

The course was at RAF Valley, on Anglesey which is where the UK's fast jet pilots learn their trade. For months beforehand I swatted up on everything to do with the Hawk, living and breathing the aircraft as much as I could. I had a cardboard cockpit at home and I'd run through all the checks in my living room and fly missions as if I was in the air. Mandy had graduated in the Hawk from RAF Valley on her way to becoming a Tornado pilot, so she passed on plenty of tips.

I knew all the emergency profiles and procedures before I even got there. Preparation for me was everything, I just didn't want to look stupid or, arguably worse, like I hadn't put in the effort when it was entirely in my own hands. I knew this was my one shot at flying a fast jet and I wasn't going to waste it, especially after SMAC 309. This was potentially career-defining and the kind of door that doesn't open to everyone.

My circuitous journey had brought me meandering around the bend and the door was slightly ajar for me. I intended to barge through.

After my first trip in the front seat with an instructor in the back, he casually asked if I was here doing the Hawk refresher course. No, no, I laughed, this is my first ever time in the front seat, I'm just very keen and very prepared. I was paired with a Tornado F3 guy, who was doing a refresher on the Hawk. He was uber confident and I sensed the instructors were more receptive to me, perhaps because they could tell I had put in so much work and didn't exude an air of superiority.

Whatever his story, they were the making of me and created the environment in which I thrived. I felt like I was riding a wave of goodwill to the finish line. They weren't going to pass me for being a nice guy, but in stark contrast to the SMAC 309 instructors, it felt like they really wanted me to do well and helped me to perform at my best to achieve my dream.

The Hawk is my absolute favourite aircraft, powerful, fast, agile and simple to fly, like driving a stunning sports car with plenty of grunt under the hood, sublime handling and killer looks. As I gained more experience in the Hawk I worked with Fighter Controller school, helping train pilots in aerial combat, also known as dog-fighting, or carrying out ship attacks at very low level. We'd fly in at fifty feet over the sea (it increased to 100 feet after a serious accident), sometimes swooping down from under the wing of a civilian Falcon trainer jet to simulate missiles inbound on a navy warship to see how the ship's crew coped with such scenarios. The flying was phenomenal and I just couldn't wait to go into work every day.

Flying the Hawk was the best job I ever had.

I like drumming. I am a drummer. Well, in the sense that I bash the drums while some music is playing, I am. I'm getting much better at it but in a way, I don't want to be brilliant (I do), I am enjoying the journey too much.

Part of it is closing my eyes in my spare bedroom and imagining I'm the beating heart of a brilliant, rocking band, driving the songs with my perfect rhythm and thunderous beat, hands a blur as I flash around the kit, a flamboyant smash of the cymbals here, a nifty fill around the tom-toms there, feet tapping out a tight tempo on the bass drum and the hi-hat, twirling my sticks like a wizard with a pair of wands. A large part of it though, is the learning with my teacher Glenn. He's a great example of a trainer or a leader creating the right environment.

"What do you know about drumming?" he asked at the start of my first taster lesson.

"Absolutely nothing."

"That's OK because by the end of this you'll be able to name five drums, you'll be able to read a bit of music and you'll be playing along to your favourite tune."

That's a big ask but it sounds great. Yes please.

I was immediately hooked. He also said I had to have fun otherwise I would be wasting my time. Glenn quickly understood my way of learning and adopted his training to suit. If he sees me struggling on something, he'll smile a bit, I'll smile back and he won't force it.

He knows I'll go home and practise ferociously to get it right for next week. When I return, he'll say, "Go on, then," and I'll whack out whatever it is we were working on. Sometimes I get it right, sometimes I don't. He'll laugh at my incompetence and I'll laugh back, happy in the environment he's created where I can fail and not mind.

Of course, mucking up a drum solo is not quite the same as making a dog's breakfast of your first solo flight. That could have far greater consequences, clearly, but the philosophy of the environment he's created is the powerful bit.

As an airline captain there have been countless situations when engaging the team, creating the right environment for them to perform and empowering them has paid serious dividends. In the airlines you rarely fly with the same people every time, so when you first meet up in the crew room you very quickly need to develop a high-performing team for the safety of that flight and for the people on board. Whether I'm training in the simulator or flying as a captain I'll never just smash straight into the briefing.

I'll always spend some time just asking about the people on the team, showing interest, finding out a bit about them, what's on their minds, essentially setting the right tone and creating the environment I want us to work in. At EasyJet it was even factored into timings and known as the 'Golden Five Minutes'. Only once we've broken the ice and everyone's happy, will I ask, "Are you ready to brief?" I'll go through the weather, the routing and any other key issues about the flight but an essential ingredient of the briefing would be a call to action. Stating that if anyone on the crew has a problem, sees something amiss or even just has a nagging doubt, they are to raise it.

I might be the captain responsible for that aircraft, but I don't want to hear from any more clones, I want to hear a different voice, and I want to be challenged.

Once I was flying a four-sector day on the Airbus A320

with a young cadet as the first officer who was going to be performing his first landing with passengers onboard when we came back into London Gatwick from Amsterdam. He touched us down without a fault but on the taxiway to the terminal I sensed a very faint judder. Sometimes you do inadvertently taxi over the centre lights, and I just put it down to him being a bit clumsy on the controls. I'm not sure the passengers would have felt anything to be alarmed about.

I was starting to think ahead to the next sector as we had a twenty-minute turnaround, and time being money in the airline world I was already plotting our next tasks. Once we had parked up and the passengers had disembarked, the senior cabin crew member approached me in the cockpit.

"You know you said in the Golden Five to raise anything, no matter how small, well I've just got this funny feeling that something is not quite right with the aircraft."

"Okay, great, thanks."

After a flight, the pilots tend take it in turns to walk around the aircraft, to check everything is serviceable and in good order for the next one and on this occasion it was the first officer's turn, but after having the faintest of whisperings of an issue myself, now backed up by the crew member, I decided I would go out and have a look myself. I began at the main landing gear and shone my torch over the outside of the tyres which looked fine. But peering closer the torch beam picked up the glint of metal embedded in the inside tyre which was deflated.

I checked all the other wheels and the fuselage and it all seemed fine, so I went back up to the cockpit and radioed ground control to tell them and they closed the main runway for a few minutes to conduct a sweep. I talked them back into the taxiway and they found the end of a towing arm, which we had clearly driven over. Our next flight was delayed while they replaced our tyre but if it hadn't been for the cabin crew member speaking up, empowered by the environment we had created, it could have been a very different outcome. Thinking about it now, the cultural environment that existed within other pockets of the airport environment appeared severely lacking.

It seems inconceivable that the person who had damaged the towing arm would be unaware of their actions and had not felt empowered to speak up and admit their mistake so a sweep could have been made before we happened to drive over it.

Another time on the Airbus, I was training a new first officer and we had a training standards captain with us to make sure my teaching was up to scratch, which added an extra layer of internal pressure. It was the final leg of a tiring four-sector day, heading from Gatwick up to Edinburgh and back. It was dark and the weather was bitter and we were already late. To manage the workload the training captain asked if he could help out with anything.

Grateful, I asked him to check the wings for ice. He went back down into the main cabin to take a look out of the windows and completed an external walk around the aircraft. He came back saying there was no need to de-ice, it all looked fine.

On this airfield you had to de-ice on the stand rather than on the taxiway so this would have delayed us even more and probably made us lose our slot causing even bigger ramifications.

Relieved that we could press on, I started the engines and we pushed back off the stand. At this point, the intercom from the cabin crew came to life.

"Hi Craig, I know I'm not supposed to call you now unless it's an emergency, but you did say in the briefing that if we had any concerns to please let you know."

"Sure, no problem, what's up?" I said.

"Do we need to de-ice?" she asked me point blank.

I told her the training captain had been to look and he thought it was fine. But here's the good bit, she didn't accept that.

"That's fine, but I'm just telling you what I can see, and I think there is a build-up of ice on the wing."

"Okay, brilliant, thanks for that. We'll take a look."

I sent the training captain back down to have another look, and he came back nodding, saying we needed to de-ice. It's not a blame game, conditions had changed so it was now the right decision, albeit a massive hassle as we had to go back on the stand and duly missed our slot. The great thing about this incident was that the cabin crew member not only had the presence of mind to speak up about her concerns but also was not afraid to challenge me as the captain. I'd said in the Golden Five to voice any concerns and I'd opened the door for people to ask me questions.

I didn't do it to tick a box because I'd once read a leadership manual, I did it because it was the right thing to do, for the team to operate effectively and ultimately for the safety of all on board. I wanted to hear from the whole team because everyone has a viewpoint and, on this occasion, it proved highly valuable. She was spot on in terms of her language and her assertive behaviour. We wouldn't have fallen out of the sky, but you definitely can't ignore the need to de-ice the wings, no matter how inconvenient it might be to your plans.

CHAPTER 5

TURBULENCE AHEAD

MANDY: What are your threats? What could cause you turbulence in your path right now? It might be a daunting exam, a hard deadline, a tough sales environment, a scheming colleague, an awkward boss or the whims of a tricky client. Maybe it's something bigger such as restructuring or redundancy or just that nagging sense that something's off. Threats are the things outside your control that can throw a spanner in the works. In flying, we're trained to spot and manage threats constantly.

In peacetime, the threats might be dodgy weather, birds near the runway, kit going wrong, or navigating airspace you shouldn't be in. Then there's the human element such as mistakes, fatigue, poor communication. All of these can tip a normal flight into what we call an Undesirable Aircraft State (UAS) which is not good. That's why we spend so long training and then preparing daily to mitigate these threats.

Of course, aviation has distinctly more jeopardy than the average job, but it is still worth looking around and being prepared. So, in your world, what are the things right now that could throw you off course or put you in an UAS? And how might you deal with potential threats as you try to alter your flight path?

Some threats you can see coming, like a storm building on the horizon. Others sneak up on you out of nowhere, like a last-minute curveball from a client. And then there are the stealthy ones, the latent threats like fatigue, stress, clunky systems, team dynamics.

They sit there, under the surface, waiting for just the right moment to trip you up. In aviation, we live by the mantra: avoid, trap, mitigate. First, you try to avoid the threat by planning thoroughly, plotting a course around the storm, checking equipment and systems work and briefing the team and making sure they are ready and fit to fly. If you can't avoid it, you trap it.

That might be spotting a fuel leak early and acting fast, following a checklist and doing exactly what the manual says. If it's too late for that, you mitigate to reduce the impact. This might be deploying oxygen masks in the cabin if pressure is lost or diverting a flight when something's gone wrong. And when things do go sideways, it is how we respond that matters.

Some unanticipated events might cause us a bit of surprise initially, but we quickly recover.

The next level up is when we're startled. This could be as simple as when the doorbell goes and you're not expecting it. Again, you regain your composure almost immediately. But shock, that's when you freeze.

It's when the emotional side of the brain takes over, what American psychologist Daniel Goleman calls the amygdala hijack. It's a very basic human emotion, stemming back to the dawn of humankind. When a hungry bear entered the cave, some people froze or panicked, others ran away, some shooed it back out. The key is to be able to respond with the rational side of your brain to achieve the most effective outcome.

Panic, or in the case of a ravenous bear, freezing is rarely the best option. In the military, we train and drill and rehearse over and over, until the right response becomes second nature. You need to stay cool, maintain your situational awareness and respond. The same goes for work and life.

Firing back an angry email or raising your voice in an emotional response is rarely an effective solution and can have a negative impact on your future path. You can't always control the storm, but you can absolutely choose how you tackle it.

When I was training on the operational conversion unit on the Tornado GR1 at RAF Lossiemouth in Scotland, we had the chance for ten days of flying out of Goose Bay in northern Canada. It was a dream trip for many but still gives me nightmares about how close I came to the end. On one particular day the threat profile was high, with thunderclouds in the air, pressure to get in one more dogfight for the trip to count as a trainee and a runway that we had been warned would be too slick to land on one side if it was wet.

Stick to the right side of the runway, where a series of ridges had been designed to dispel water, was the mitigating advice. Then add in that I was flying on fumes as I came in to land after all the ducking and diving of aerial combat, and a trainee air traffic controller talking me down through the clouds. It was the classic Swiss cheese model, as devised by Professor James Reason, where layers of cheese are stacked up, with each slice providing a defence against errors. The holes in the cheese represent weakness in the system.

When the holes all line up, major errors can occur. On this day the holes were aligned and delivered an actual, terrifying event. As I descended through the clouds, I was becoming confused by the trainee's instructions, sensing something was off. As the runway emerged out of the clag, I realised I was badly offline and I yanked the stick over to avoid the parked jets on the apron.

Now I was lined up with the centre line of the runway and looking good. But in my haste, I'd forgotten the instructions to avoid the left and centre in the wet. Too late. My wheels touched down and the jet immediately started aquaplaning sideways at speed.

Bloody hell.

"Loss of directional control," urged my navigator over the intercom.

It was the standard response we practised repeatedly for such an occasion. Although I was probably in startle mode, I was able to function and apply the correct drills as the training dictated, performing a textbook procedure of cancelling thrust reverse and selecting idle. The trouble was, we were still going sideways at a rate of knots. Flipping heck...

They say don't knock things until you've tried them but sliding sideways on a concrete runway at 150 knots in a Tornado is not worth trying out. I had no control over the jet and just sat there staring ahead, as I accepted my fate.

"I'm not ejecting yet." That was my nav again.

Crikey, are we going to have to eject? I hadn't even thought of that. That is not going to end well.

Eventually, we skidded towards the right side of the runway where the series of corrugations began to slow us down. After we had come to a stop, I reopened the throttles to move off the runway but instead of easing forwards we roared backwards, like a pensioner in a car park selecting reverse instead of first gear.

"What the hell...?" I cried.

"Mandy, you've still got reverse thrust on from the landing."

"Oh yes, good point."

My mental capacity was maxed out and I was in the shock phase, reacting emotionally with no situational awareness whatsoever.

Threats can be short-lived or have long-term consequences and come from the most unexpected places. At a recent Pendulum Summit, one of my tasks was to interview Wim Hof, aka 'The Iceman'. The Dutchman is a famous extreme athlete with a remarkable ability to withstand cold temperatures. When I met Wim backstage, I explained that I knew a bit about the subject given my dissertation at university was on cold water immersion and the initial gasp reflex.

I wanted to build a quick connection and give him the idea that I was a worthy interviewer. Once on stage under the bright lights it started okay, but then Wim began to ignore my questions and started playing some bongos he had brought with him and doing the splits, live in front of two thousand people. A feeling of dread flooded my chest as humiliation, and a public Undesirable Aircraft State was looking a distinct possibility. Inside my head, the cogs were whirring faster than ChatGPT spewing out an answer as I weighed up how to respond.

Subconsciously, I opted for humour to try to trap this growing threat. I stood up and pretended to walk off, hoping to style it out but petrified no one would notice or Wim wouldn't call me back, like pretending to walk out of a shop after an unsuccessful attempt at haggling, desperately hoping they will call you back and agree to your price. Fortunately, before I had walked too far and had to start thinking about a plan B, Wim did call me back. He was a model interviewee after that.

Threat just about averted.

Sometimes threats can be of our own making. A classic one is thinking you've got just about enough petrol to get there and zooming past the motorway services, even though your fuel gauge is nudging towards the red zone. Then you spend the next twenty miles sweating and panicking that you are going to run out and you've made a big mistake (again) and when will you ever learn and how are you going to fill up while stuck on the hard shoulder and how are you going to explain this one, and do the AA even do emergency petrol runs?.

Early in my speaking career I was guilty of over committing, keen to please everyone, to establish myself on the circuit, to earn some money and build a business. Once, I had agreed to speak at a fundraiser for a hospice on the south coast of England. My sister is a medical director of a hospice, so it is a cause close to my heart. But then another opportunity came in to speak at a major aeronautical engineering company in the north of England earlier the same day.

I looked at the trains and the timings just about worked, even though I knew the margins for error were razor thin. I gambled – She who dares, wins and all that – and accepted. The first engagement went fine but the UK transport system and the British weather did their best to scupper me on my dash south with trains cancelled, missed connections, taxis unavailable and gridlocked roads. Even though I preach it, I had ignored the golden rule that 'just about' should be a warning sign flashing in neon.

In the air, 'just about' is a complete no-no because the consequences are too dire, but on the ground, we tend to stretch that envelope, creating threats of our own making and ending up in all manner of pickles. At each setback on my crazy dash down south I had to recalibrate my plan, balancing risk, reward and the reality of time slipping away. Through a combination of trains, taxis and eventually my own car, I made the hospice with two minutes to spare, applying some lipstick as I hot-footed it from the car park. She dared and won, you could say, but in terms of threat management there was plenty still to learn.

Tootling about the inky night sky above southern Iraq on a routine patrol I let my mind wander. We were out and about to remind the Iraqis that we were still very interested and were fully loaded with weapons should they try any shenanigans, but nothing much happened down here over the desert anyway. All seemed well and I was thinking of home. Just a few days until the end of my tour of the Gulf with II (AC) squadron.

I let my shoulders relax away from the straps pinning me into my ejection seat and stretched each leg as much as I could in the confines of the cramped cockpit. I had the green glow of my head-up display for company, the ever-present purr of the Tornado's twin engines in my ear despite the tight fit of my helmet and the knowledge that my navigator Jacko was in the back seat scanning his screens. The faint outline of my wingman Stinger a mile to my right reminded me I wasn't alone. My mind drifted to the mundane pleasures waiting at home, such as wandering around the shops, strolling down Winchester high street, popping out for coffee, seeing the girls for a catch-up.

"BREAK RIGHT..."

Jacko's voice in my headset sent a surge of electricity through my body and yanked my mind from its daydream, thrusting it back inside the cockpit. I'd heard the command before, of course. I'd trained relentlessly for this moment and instinctively I rocked the stick to the right with my right hand and thrust the throttles forward with my left. I tensed my stomach muscles, ready to accept the punch that was coming from the G-suit to keep my blood flowing and stop me blacking out.

"Missile lock, five o'clock..." Jacko's voice again, straining now as the G-force of the turn kicked in.

And then a blinding flash behind us, like a ball of white lightning. Jacko had deployed flares; millions of slivers of metal designed to intercept the missile and confuse it into exploding, while we roared away into the Iraqi night sky like a cat with its tail on fire. We'd mitigated the threat by releasing the chaff and having an instinctive procedure ingrained through hours and hours of training. It startled me, but there was no panic, no freezing, no, "Oh shit, we're in trouble" or worse, just a professional, ingrained response to a known, if not entirely expected threat.

The idea that someone on the ground is trying, actually, for real and not in a training exercise, to blow you out of the sky is quite profound when you think about it later. Why me? I'm just Mandy. What will my mum say? But when you're up there in your multi-million-pound jet poised to wreak havoc you're RAF enemy number one with a target on your belly. On this occasion, the threat was high.

Life-threatening in fact. But the holes in the Swiss cheese didn't line up, we performed as programmed and completed the mission.

CRAIG: We had been dogfighting above the skies of Cornwall. Me, in the backseat of the Hawk with a Sea Harrier pilot in the front going up against another pair in a Hawk, simulating the air-to-air combat reminiscent of the Battle of Britain, when Spitfires and Hurricanes scrapped with Messerschmidts and Junkers of the German Luftwaffe, whirling and twirling in deadly duels over southern Britain. Our sortie was the stuff of the *Top Gun* films, one-on-one combat, "Yee-ha, Jester's dead! Hit the brakes, he'll fly right by" kind of stuff. It certainly wakes you up of a morning and we were fizzing as we broke off the engagement, the other Hawk returning to base at RNAS Yeovilton and us heading down to low level to wind up through Wales to land at RAF Valley on Anglesey to take a simulator refresher session.

Flying at 420 knots (around 485mph) at 250 feet above the ground through twisting, narrow valleys makes for a rip-roaring ride, like being fired down a human marble run. We knew the route reasonably well so it was fairly routine, but you can't be complacent as the workload is quite high with turning points to factor in. As the back-seater, I wasn't flying the airplane, so I sat with my hands on my knees, rolling with the jet and watching the green valley walls flash by above us.

And then... BANG! A huge thud from the front left side of the jet followed by ricochets all around the airframe. What the...? The engine's pitch changed to a high whine as it sucked for air and scrambled for power, like trying to breathe inside a plastic bag. Bird strike. And we're not talking about a robin either, this was big, maybe a stork.

With all that bone and feathers inside it, the engine was straining. If it continued to surge it could blow itself up.

The first thing to do in this instance is to get away from low level and convert speed to height. In any instance like this, flying the aircraft is the first priority: aviate, navigate, communicate.

Next, and we're talking instantly, you need to close the throttles to shut off the airflow to allow the engine to stabilise and hopefully stop the surge. If that doesn't fix it, you go for an engine shut down and immediate relight. Shutting down the engine, of course, means the aircraft is now effectively a glider at 420 knots which brings with it another set of issues, but the hope is that a relight will unblock the airflow and the engine will be okay again. I sensed the nose of the aircraft lifting but the guy in the front seat was quiet, surprised certainly (we weren't expecting this), startled probably, shock possibly, could even be frozen. These are all very normal responses to a sudden drama.

I looked down the cockpit and could see the tip of his helmet above his ejection seat. His head was motionless. He was technically the captain of this ship, but it was clear something was up. Maybe I could help.

"Engine is in surge!" I stated with a sense of urgency.

Come on, buddy, talk to me. Maybe he's just being slow to respond, I thought, but milliseconds were ticking by. I could see, hear and feel we were in surge but maybe he hadn't picked it up, or worse was in shock and frozen, unable to function. Maybe I was slightly more detached because I was in the back and slightly removed from the impact and the spattering of blood on the canopy, or because I wasn't the captain with overall responsibility.

Whatever, there's no machismo, no heroics, no blame, it's just that on this occasion I had processed the information quicker than the driver and recognised we needed to act to get out of a potentially lethal situation. The first thing that went through my mind was I'm not really up for ejecting today, any day in fact. Ejecting safely from a jet is never a given and being over six feet tall with long legs I was conscious I might kneecap myself on the Hawk's coaming as I fired myself out of the speeding cockpit.

Oh dear, this is not good.

"Close the throttle," I urged. More seconds passed. The valley walls were scrolling past and our engine was screaming.

"Mate, close the throttle!" My insistent voice matched the high pitch of the engine. I could feel the throttle was now back at idle, but the engine did not respond, it was still in surge.

I tried again: "Shut down the engine, immediate relight."

And then I heard the engine die to nothing... a tense pause in which time stood still... and then the roar of the relight, one of the sweetest sounds I'd ever heard. You absolute flipping beauty.

"You alright up there?"

"Yep, sorry... I'm fine. Just..."

The truth was, he was probably unable to process the information as quickly as you would normally expect. The shock of the bird strike had brought out an emotional response, rather than an automatic reaction. It's natural and can happen to anyone but that's why we train so hard to mitigate these threats. Not that we were out of the woods though.

The engine still wasn't right, and we couldn't try to push on to Valley. Our priority was to get the jet onto the ground quickly. I got on the radio, breathing heavily, my voice strained and insistent, imploring.

"Mayday, mayday, mayday, Bronze Two, Hawk, engine failure, relit, heading west, altitude 6,000ft, two POB [persons on board], request immediate diversion to Llanbedr." It was the first and only time I've ever put out a mayday call.

Llanbedr airfield in west Wales was nearby but, like any reasonable military establishment on a Friday, it had closed for lunch. Fortunately, someone was home and monitoring the emergency channels and when they heard the mayday we were directed to land. We set up for a practised forced landing, something we were very used to from training and essentially glided in with the throttles in idle and the flaps down. As the wheels kissed the tarmac, I felt my shoulders deflate as the tension began to drain away, like opening the valve on a blow-up mattress.

Once we had come to a stop and shut down the jet, I sat still for a few moments, just staring at the cockpit, listening to my breaths, heavy and laboured. When I had gathered myself, I patted the display panel, pulled the canopy open and climbed out. Taking my helmet off on the tarmac I waited for the front seater. After he had made his way down from the cockpit we hugged.

Despite some tense moments, we had recovered well and worked as a team to get down safely.

"Close one," I said.

"Yep, good work."

"What are we going to do now?"

Breaking from our embrace we looked at the aircraft, which had a dent the size of an ironing board down the left-hand side of the fuselage and the red smear of blood all over the front left section of the canopy. Goodness knows what damage there was to the engine. We were at the wrong airfield with a sick jet and no apparent way to get home. An RAF helicopter that was in the area had heard our mayday and followed us into Llanbedr and their crew chief came over.

"You guys need a lift somewhere?"

Leaving the Hawk, we hopped into the Sea King for the short dash up the coast to Valley. By now the guys at Yeovilton had called up to cancel our sim session but I asked for it to be reinstated. I was there to do it and I wanted to get it out of the way. I could probably skip the emergency relight section as I'd just done that for real.

In hindsight I should have been told that doing a sim session wasn't a good idea as I was clearly agitated but I got through it okay and we cadged a lift home with the Heron flight in their Jetstream which was passing on its way from Prestwick in Scotland down to Yeovilton. The engine turned out to be a write-off and the airframe had a huge hole in it. An eventful day.

On another occasion, I was sitting in the cockpit of my Airbus readying for take-off from Malaga bound for Heathrow. All the passengers were on board and pushback from the stand was imminent as we had a tight fifteen-minute time slot to get airborne. Miss that, and the knock-on effect could potentially strand us there for the night. I was completing the final paperwork when I got a call from the cabin manager saying she had received concerning complaints from a couple of the passengers.

"Sure, come and tell me more," I said.

I'd flown with this cabin crew member a few times and

she was very experienced. She told me that a couple of ladies in business class, independently of each other, had spoken to her about some fellow passengers who were making them feel very nervous. It was shortly after the terrorist attacks of 9/11 and people were quite agitated about flying, for good reason. Apparently, a group of passengers, seemingly from the Middle East, were constantly getting up and down and moving things in the overhead locker.

They also kept going to the toilet, she said. She had looked in the toilet and there were clearly footprints on the seat. Blimey. Not heard that one before.

What's all this about? Were they climbing up and putting something behind a bulkhead perhaps? I listened to the story and then took a couple of moments before replying, choosing my words carefully.

"Thanks for letting me know. So, what is it they've actually done?"

Well, nothing, she replied but the point is these two passengers are very anxious. Safety was my number one priority, and as far as these ladies were concerned there was a threat to the safety of the flight. I couldn't just bat away their concerns. On the other hand, I had a group of gentlemen who had merely rearranged some luggage in the overhead locker and visited the toilet.

Was that really a threat? I was a bit flummoxed and the way forward was not obvious. I took stock and decided I had to put faith in the system. The security team and the check-in staff would have done their jobs, including performing all the necessary checks with computers and scanners. Just as I don't stand around holding the fuel nozzle in the jet, so I don't go down to the desk and do all the checking in.

I have to assume the team will do that.

I decided to work my way through the system, so I started with the dispatcher, who loaded the aircraft. I explained the complaint and asked for her thoughts. She said they'd cleared security and were five members of the extended United Arab Emirates' royal family. That established the basics and was an interesting twist, but it didn't really help me.

It shouldn't make any difference who the passengers were, but it played on my mind. Next, I asked some of the cabin crew to meet me in the cockpit.

"Guys, what are your thoughts here?".

Everyone replied that safety came first and that if we had any safety issues, we had to offload the UAE passengers. Yes, I think you're right, I said. It has to be the correct course of action. Those footprints on the toilet seat were certainly odd and I had several very anxious people on board.

But I had a nagging feeling in the back of my mind. What had they actually done wrong? I clearly needed to speak to them.

I took a deep breath and followed the cabin crew member out of the cockpit and into business class to where the men were sitting. I quickly scanned the group, one was dressed formally in a smart suit and I concluded this older gentleman, who looked to be over forty, must be the passenger I'd been told had the title 'Dr.' though I didn't know if that was a medical or academic honour. The rest were in their mid-twenties wearing the kandura, the traditional long sleeved white robes of the UAE. I put on my best smile, fixed the older guy in the eyes and spoke quietly.

"Hi, I'm Craig, I'm the captain and I am very sorry to bother you, but I'd be very grateful if you would join me just to the side of the aircraft to answer a few questions."

The senior guy, in accented but perfect English, agreed to follow me and gestured to the others to get up. Once off the aircraft I carried on.

"I'm acutely aware of who you are, and I want to be respectful, but my only concerns are the safety of this aircraft. I need to let you know that we've had concerns raised by two independent passengers regarding your behaviour. Can you help me with this? Is there anything I should know about your hand luggage in the overhead locker?"

The lead gentleman said there was no issue with their bags, they were just readying themselves for the flight.

"What is it you think we have done?" he asked.

I didn't really have an answer to this.

"Do you know anything about footprints on the toilet seats?" I ventured.

No one replied to this, and I looked around the group from man to man.

"Okay, guys thank you so much. Just to emphasise my role here – I hope I haven't embarrassed you, but again, my number one priority is the safety of aircraft. Please return to your seats."

The older passenger said he understood why I had to question them but said it was discrimination and unfair that they were being targeted. He said that I would be hearing from him and insisted on taking my name.

That didn't bother me, but I still hadn't made a decision on how to proceed. I knew this was going to be a big call either way. The safest course of action must be to offload them. Why would you not do that? There was a big flashing threat and the easiest way to avoid it would be to take them off the flight.

By now we'd missed our take-off slot, but I asked the first officer to prepare the flight deck for departure while I continued to deal with the issue. I was quite a new captain, and I couldn't get hold of anyone senior at the airline so I was on my own. Every time I thought offloading them had to be the way forward, a nagging voice in my head shouted, "Why?".

Right, Craigy, you're going to have to show some leadership here.

Reassuring myself I had made the right decision, I gathered the team around again away from passengers and explained my dilemma. I said that as there was no clear evidence of any wrongdoing or anything more suspicious than moving some bags, then if no one had any objections, I would be taking the group of UAE passengers.

I called the lead passenger into the galley and explained that we'd been through all of our checks and there was no reason not to take them. I told him we didn't mean to cause embarrassment or offence and I apologised for that. He accepted my apology but said he would be complaining to the foreign office. I only found out later that crouching on the toilet seat might have cultural relevance.

We still had the problem of the two passengers who had made the complaints. I needed to explain my decision to them. In their view the group were acting suspiciously. I appreciated their observations.

Let's face it, they could have been the people who saved the day and the lives of hundreds if their imaginary scenarios had played out. I spoke to them quietly in turn in the galley, thanking them for their observations. I said that I was satisfied everything had been done to verify the safety of the aircraft and I was happy to take the group as passengers. I asked them how they would like to proceed.

One opted to stay on the flight, the other got off.

By the time we filed for another slot and took off it was late when we got back to Heathrow. We parked up and the passengers disembarked without incident, including the royal party, who were met by a special vehicle with flashing lights. I left a message for our operations director to let him know what had happened and drove home. He called me early the following morning.

"Craig, we've had a complaint from the foreign office.

Apparently, you nearly offloaded five members of the UAE royal family.".

"Yes, I was very close."

"I'm so glad you didn't, it would have caused a diplomatic nightmare."

You can imagine the newspapers' reaction to these guys being offloaded from a flight for going to the toilet. Despite that, no one could have really criticised me for taking the safety-first route with a packed Airbus.

Sometimes threats come from so far out of left field you just cannot plan for them, but by remaining agile, open-minded and clear-headed you will be primed to tackle them head on.

Craig; All the family, with Mum, Dad, Mark, Vanessa and Paul. Washington DC.

Craig; My inspiration, my mentor, my Dad, John Hickson.

The first ever aircraft both Mandy and Craig flew. The Chipmunk was a handful on the ground but delightful in the air.

772 Naval Air Squadron: Search and Rescue. For every 'shout' we need the whole team'.

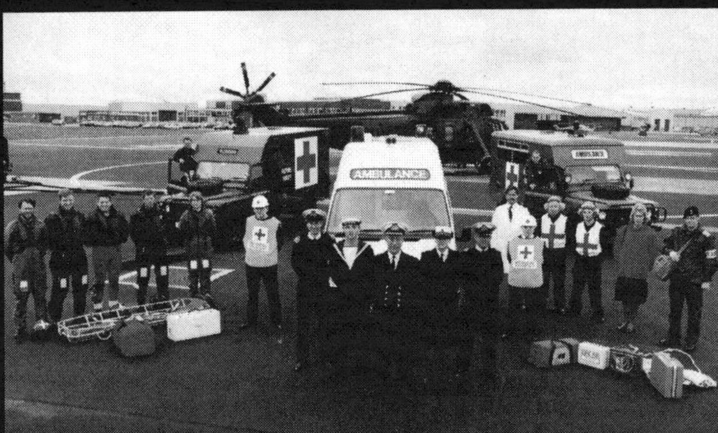

April 1986: Wings day! A proud moment for Craig and all the family.

The mighty Hawk T1, Craig's favourite aircraft ever.

The Royal Navy's black Hawk.

The Sea King Mk 4.

Mandy's first flight certificate, aged 15.

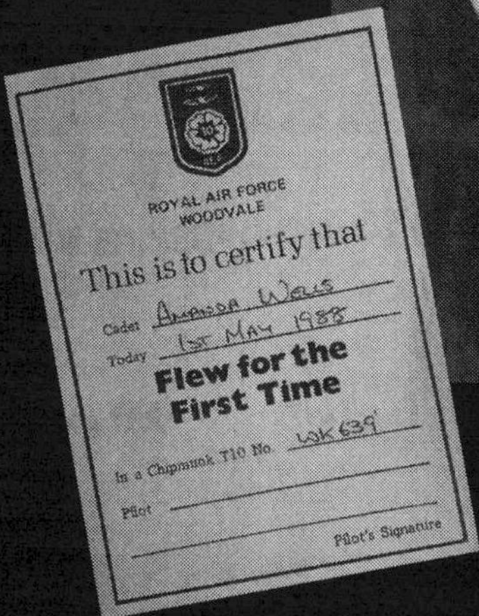

ROYAL AIR FORCE
WOODVALE

This is to certify that

Cadet Amanda Wells

Today 1st May 1988

Flew for the First Time

In a Chipmunk T10 No. WK 639

Pilot

Pilot's Signature

Mandy was awarded a Leadership award for the Northwest in 1987, aged 14.

First solo on Mandy's flying scholarship, Blackpool airport, aged 17.

Basic flying training on the Tucano.

Advanced flying training, RAF Valley.

Craig flew a Hawk in
to RAF Valley, 1998.

Mandy's Wings
parade, 1998.

RAF Valley Summer
Ball 1998.

Mandy's Wings parade, 1998: Dad, Mandy, Sarah and Mum.

Mandy's first squadron. II(AC) Sqn flying the Tornado GR4.

Mandy's first squadron. II(AC) Sqn flying the Tornado GR4.

Mandy's first squadron. II(AC) Sqn flying the Tornado GR4.

Craig: What an absolute privilege to fly and display the venerable Swordfish.

23 July 1999, Craig and crew en route to Lulworth Cove.

Our last photo of Paul Hickson, working for the United Nations, Islamabad 2006.

Mandy, Jack, Jamie and Craig at Queen Elizabeth II's Diamond Jubilee 2012.

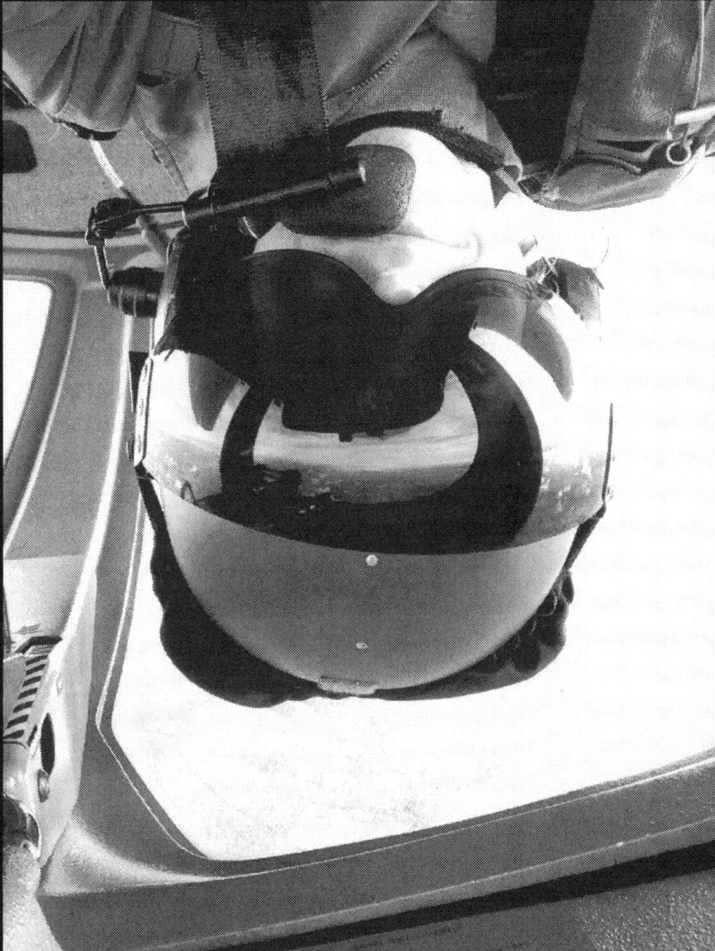

Flying cadets with 2 AEF, MOD Boscombe Down on the Tutor aircraft.

Mandy speaking at the International Atomic Energy Agency, Vienna 2015.

Great views from the best office in the world, A320.

Jack, Elliot, Chessie and Jamie, 2015.

One of Mandy's first talks to schools. Lord Wandsworth College, 2012.

The flamboyance of pilots, Kirsty Murphy, myself and Jo Salter.

Flying the Airbus A320 into Gibraltar with easyJet, 2017.

Right: Good Housekeeping Magazine, 2023.

Interview with Fred Dinenage for ITV.

Mandy becomes an Ambassador for girl guiding and gets a badge in her honour.

Craig finally gets to perform live on the drums.

Mandy as the face of the Dorchester Collection 'Legends' advertising campaign.

Remembrance Sunday, Westminster, 2022.

Mandy reaches the summit of Kilimanjaro, 2019.

Meeting Maverick (aka Tom Cruise) at the Royal International Air Tattoo in 2023.

Mandy hosting the Pendulum Summit as MC, Dublin, 2022–2025.

Base Camp of Everest, 2023.

Base Camp of Everest, 2023.

Donating all moneys raised on the expedition to Winchester Hospice.

Backpacking around Vietnam with Jack and Jamie, 2024.

Mum, Mandy and Sarah, 2025.

Our happy place,
The Pyrenees.

Duke of Edinburgh's
Award presentations,
Buckingham Palace,
2025.

Jamie and Mandy at Buckingham Palace, 2025.

Mandy was awarded The Champion of Women award at the Veterans in business awards, 2025.

Back to the skies,
single engine
piston flying, 2025.

RIAT, 2025.

Interviewing Tim Peake on the Inspire stage at the RIAT.

Mandy presenting all over the world, Munich, 2025.

The journey continues...
Roys Peak, New Zealand,
2025.

CHAPTER 6

BUZZING THE TOWER

MANDY: In the original *Top Gun* movie, Maverick is pumped up after beating his instructor Jester in a training mission. He gets on the radio and asks air traffic control for permission to "buzz the tower", or fly low over the airfield, to celebrate.

"Tower, this is Ghostrider requesting a flyby."

"Negative Ghostrider, the pattern is full."

It's a classic line and to this day I still often use it to mean no. The scene is designed to show Maverick's reckless side by requesting a dangerous, low-level pass over a busy airfield with other jets landing and taking off. It is also useful in showing how human beings are a crucial element in any system, and that human error is a big player in the threat world. Despite being told no and urged it wasn't a good idea by his backseater Goose, Maverick buzzed the tower anyway.

It could have had serious repercussions, but this being Hollywood and Tom Cruise being Maverick, it turned out the only issue was the guy in the tower spilling his coffee down his shirt from the thunderous vibrations of the F-14 Tomcat.

It is important to stress that everyone makes mistakes. It is an inconvenient but fundamental part of being human. And it is true whether you're a pilot, a surgeon, a bricklayer or an office intern. I've never met anyone who goes to work wanting to make a mistake, to deliberately mess things up.

Even Maverick wasn't trying to crash his jet. But stuff happens with people, and it is how you as an individual react and how companies, through their culture, deal with it. Adapting your mindset to mistakes and using them as an opportunity to review the bigger picture is a flex that will put you on a par with the highest-performing teams.

When cockpit voice recorders were introduced to aircraft in the 1970s it became clear that human errors played a large part in aviation accidents. Analysis of the tapes showed that many of those errors came down to issues with interpersonal skills, communication, decision-making and leadership, rather than fundamental flying competency. The Tenerife airport disaster of 1977 was a case in point, when two Boeing 747 airliners collided on the runway in thick fog, resulting in 583 fatalities. A KLM flight began its take-off run, thinking it had clearance, but a Pan Am aircraft was still on the runway taxiing to exit the strip after landing.

The KLM jet managed to lift its front wheels, but it was too late and it hit the other aircraft. The impact, crash and ensuing fire killed all of those on board the KLM flight and most of those on the Pan Am jet, with only sixty-one survivors in the front section. It was a classic example of the hazard holes lining up. A bomb in the terminal at Gran Canaria had diverted many aircraft to Tenerife so the airfield was congested, with planes taxiing on the runway.

The fog was also a major threat with neither aircraft visible to each other or the tower, and there was no ground radar. But investigators focused on the communication between both flight decks and air traffic control. From the harrowing final snippets of conversation from the cockpit voice recorders they deemed the tragedy stemmed from vague, non-standard language, with instructions and replies misinterpreted. Radio interference at a crucial moment contributed to the KLM crew thinking they were in the clear.

The dynamics on the KLM flight deck were also questioned, with the captain appearing to disregard input from others.

Another incident fuelling the need for more work on the human factors side was the crash of United Airlines Flight 173 on December 28, 1978. The DC-8 aircraft was flying from John F Kennedy Airport in New York to Portland, Oregon when the crew experienced a problem with the landing gear. The captain decided to fly a holding pattern outside Portland to investigate the issue, but he became so absorbed in trying to fix the gear that he failed to notice the fuel was fast diminishing, despite the warnings of the first officer and flight engineer. The jet eventually ran out of fuel and crash-landed in the suburbs of Portland.

Of the 181 people on board, two crew and eight passengers lost their lives. The subsequent inquiry noted that alongside the captain's loss of situational awareness, the lack of assertiveness of the crew members and deference to the captain, who appeared transfixed with his gear, was a significant factor in the tragedy.

The study of human psychology is as old as time – picture those early cave dwellers Og and Ug trying to work out whether Ag was going to steal the last piece of woolly mammoth meat. But analysing these incidents and many others led human factors experts to spawn the discipline of cockpit resource management (CRM), which was later broadened to crew resource management to encompass anyone with an operational input on a flight, including air traffic control.

When I left the RAF and was searching around for a future direction, I took a training course in CRM. I found all the human factors elements and how to manage the threats fascinating. I loved how people and their behaviours can be so intrinsic to a system and how a change in mindset can produce a very different outcome. I enjoyed it so much I became a facilitator, helping to qualify CRM trainers from around the globe in aviation and medicine.

CRM works on the premise that everyone makes mistakes. In aviation that can be aircraft handling errors, procedural errors, as well as social and communication errors. It then seeks to manage this threat with better training in cognitive, communication and social skills to improve onboard safety, with an open and transparent culture encouraged to share the learning.

Human errors can take various forms, all subtly different but all capable of shoving a great big stick through the spokes. You will have umpteen examples from your life and career when individuals were at fault. Some are just blatantly deliberate such as driving over the speed limit or cutting corners to accomplish a task more quickly. Others are deliberate actions but mistaken in their execution such as operating your windscreen wipers in your car when you meant to flick on the indicators.

Then there are lapses when you inadvertently fail to perform the required action, such as not looking in your mirror before pulling out. In 1947, before human factors became a big thing, Fitts and Jones published a paper investigating the recurring mistakes of World War II pilots. In certain aircraft, pilots were all too often lowering or raising the landing gear when they should have been operating the flaps and vice versa. Fitts and Jones suggested these were not isolated slips or intended actions gone wrong, although you could argue they were both, but a problem baked into the whole system: the levers for both controls looked alike and were next to each other.

So, while it was the pilots' responsibility to operate the aircraft, the error could be seen to be a latent threat left by the designer.

Delving deeper into the topic, some human errors are caused by cognitive bias, which is a person's tendency to judge their environment and make decisions based on their personal experience or preferences. It is not always negative – gut feeling is a good example. But often cognitive bias can get you into trouble. Expectation bias is one example, where people react based on what they think they've seen or expect to have seen, not what actually exists.

When coming into land, pilots will announce "three greens" to indicate they have three green lights showing the landing gear on the nose, left and right sides are down and locked. A red light would be a major flag, but it is all too easy for the pilot to reel off "three greens" without really stopping to check whether they actually have three green lights displayed.

A famous instance of this was the fatal crash of the Delta Boeing 727 at Dallas Fort Worth in 1989. A review of the cockpit voice recorder revealed the first officer replying to the checklist challenge item "Flaps?" with "Fifteen, fifteen, green light." This would have been the correct response if the flaps had been set correctly for take-off, but it turns out they weren't. The inquiry stated that one of the contributors to the crash was a non-sterile cockpit with crew distracted by non-operational chatter.

A big threat in the airline industry is inadvertent slide deployment where the emergency escape slides are set off accidentally when the aircraft is on stand. These giant inflatables blow out of the side of the aircraft in less than ten seconds and doing it inadvertently could cause damage, injury and even death if someone was to be knocked off a jetty. There is also the cost involved to the business in repacking the slide and having to cancel or delay the flight. According to figures from human factors specialists Jarvis Bagshaw, airlines were suffering at least one deployment every 75,000 sectors on the Airbus A320.

EasyJet was experiencing at least five per year up to 2013. For the slides to fire, the door must be opened while it is still armed and operational procedures were in place to make sure the cabin crew didn't open the door inadvertently. The problem was that the procedures were failing all too often. So, EasyJet turned to Dr Steven Jarvis, the editor of the weighty UK aviation industry CRM manual *CAP 737*, who conducted an in-depth study of the process the cabin crew went through to disarm the doors before opening them on stand.

He concluded the procedure was too routine and crews were becoming complacent and not really thinking about what they were doing. In other words, expectation bias. They assumed the doors would be safe to open because they normally were. He concluded it wasn't just the random errors of numerous individuals but another example of a latent threat in the system.

Jarvis introduced stop-check measures to break the automation. The process now required two cabin crew; one crew member provided a silent physical barrier in the form of their hand covering the opening handle until the other crew member disarms the door. This was visual and quiet to minimise the chance of expectation bias. His intervention reduced ISD to zero between 2013 and 2023.

Industry rates dropped to below one in a million sectors.

During my early days of flying training with the RAF I experienced a gut-wrenching example of expectation bias. It was the day of my first solo flight in the Tucano and because our home airfield Linton was quite busy, I had flown up to Dishforth with my examiner Wing Commander Orwell. I brought the aircraft to a stop and followed the correct procedure by putting in the pins to stop my ejection seat from firing when I didn't want it to. That would have been inconvenient at best.

He got out to watch my first solo flight from the air traffic control tower and I set off again, flying numerous circuits to show him what a whizz I was before landing to go and hear the good news. Except that when I was shutting down the jet, I realised I had left the ejection seat pins in, which meant that if I had needed to exit at altitude it wouldn't have worked and I would have been a goner. I weaved as I walked across the tarmac to the tower, as if I'd had one sherry too many, as the enormity of my cock-up hit home. Because we were at a new airfield and because the workload and pressure were higher and because there was a breakdown from my standard procedures, these additional distractions meant that I hadn't performed my checks properly.

The expectation bias was that it would be the same as it always was. Embarrassed, I hid the mistake like a naughty schoolgirl hiding a guilty secret.

Looking at my Dishforth incident through a human factors lens, my misadventures were begging to be dissected. In hindsight it was a classic example of a culture where a young pilot going through a highly competitive training environment didn't feel like she could feed back openly on what had happened and the circumstances surrounding it, for fear of embarrassment or reprisal. I just didn't feel like I could or should share what I had done. The environment was such that I thought it would jeopardise my career.

The Goose Bay incident, when I lost directional control on the runway, is another example where there should have been a wider enquiry, not just a chat over a cup of tea. There were so many mitigating reasons behind why the incident had happened and feeding back could have helped prevent someone else experiencing the same incident, or possibly worse. Fortunately, no one did. Again, I should have spoken up, escalated it, but I didn't feel like the culture at the time was set up for it.

With my CRM work on top of my aviation experience I set about trying to cement my career as a speaker. It seemed that every time I asked an organisation what they would like me to talk about it always came back to the same core areas: leadership, decision-making, teamwork and culture. The same areas we focus on in CRM training to keep us safe in the air, are exactly the areas that businesses want to hone in on for a better working environment and higher profitability. I started to run targeted workshops, initially for high-risk industries like the oil and gas sector, energy, medicine and police forces.

One of the most memorable was running three sessions in one day for a chemical plant in Hull. I had covered the morning and afternoon slots and was going back in at 9pm for the night shift. I was already tired after a long day, and when I walked into the room, I felt my reserves of energy nudging into the red. There were 19 men and one woman, all dressed in bright orange personal protective equipment, sitting with their arms folded tightly across their chests, a look on their faces as if to say "What on earth can this fast jet pilot teach me?"

I took a deep breath, gave myself a quick mental kick up the backside, and launched into a case study of Elaine Bromley who died while undergoing a routine nasal operation in March 2009. Tragically, after an aborted attempt to perform the operation Elaine died after her airway had not been stabilised. As I related the tale I could see I had captured their attention. The causal factors that were identified in an investigation after Elaine's death were poor leadership and decision-making, lack of situational awareness and communication barriers.

It was a story close to my heart as her husband Martin Bromley is an airline captain and CRM trainer himself. The human factors at play in that operating theatre were very relevant to each and every one of the chemical plant engineers in that room.

I then went on to ask the simple question, "In the event of an emergency in an aircraft, who flies the airplane?"

Everyone answered, "The captain". But this is not normally the case. It would not be unusual for the captain to hand over control of the aircraft to the first officer while they assess the bigger picture. I left them to think about it.

Two years after this training session I received an email from one of the engineers who wanted to let me know that he had been the supervisor on shift the previous night when an emergency had taken place. He rushed into the control room and was about to take over when he remembered our discussions. He stopped himself, took a physical step back and spotted something that he would have missed if he had taken hands-on control. He wanted to let me know that the training that I had shared with their team had prevented an escalation of the emergency that night.

Another notable session was with the leadership teams from two police forces. I started by asking if they were happy to share any mistakes they had made. A stony silence. You could almost see the tumbleweed blowing across the room...

I let the silence sit in the air. I wanted it to be memorable. We then ran the interactive session, discussing culture, reporting and the fact that for every one major event (in the aviation sector that's normally a crash with loss of life), there will be 29 minor incidents when a report must be submitted. But there will also be 300 near misses which largely go unreported.

Years after, Heinrich put forward the pyramid in his book *Industrial Accident Prevention: A Scientific Approach*, Frank E Bird developed it into the accident triangle commonly seen today.

When people are asked why they didn't report an incident or near miss, it's often because it was not deemed important enough, what was the point, nothing would change (learned helplessness), fear of reprisals, shame and embarrassment. The 300:29:1 theory means that any accident is preventable. If we can identify the unsafe behaviour patterns that we all fall into, we can avoid any accident. I went on to ask if they had any fantastic 300 events that they could share.

The floodgates opened and brilliant learning points were captured. So, it turns out that those 300 events are the same as mistakes. It's just how we frame it. Since that session I have visited many police departments and been met with a triangle with '1:30:300 on it. What's been your latest 300 event?'

Aviation is perhaps at the vanguard of threat and error management because there is so much more at stake, but high-performing teams and smart organisations also adopt this mentality. They adopt a 'just' culture and recognise that looking for someone to blame isn't useful. They embrace every mistake as a learning opportunity and encourage openness about errors to add to the information bank. Their methodology is to identify the issue, the weak spot in the system at any given moment and find a mechanism to deal with it.

That's not to say people shouldn't be accountable for their actions, particularly if they are deemed reckless or deliberately harmful, but the philosophy is that pointing the finger isn't necessarily an effective way to make sure it doesn't happen again. This might be in terms of safety, but it could equally be a performance issue which once sorted will benefit the bottom line.

If you are in a position of influence, or about to be, it is worth thinking about how 'just' your culture is. If the answer is not very, you might have discovered a leak in the system that could be harmful to the business. On a personal level, you might think you can't change a company culture, but you can choose how you respond to mistakes, either of your own making or those of others in your circle. Turning your sphere of influence into a 'just' culture could enhance performance and ultimately pay dividends for your future path.

CRAIG: As we've seen from Maverick's antics, threats can be of our own making, a function of our own actions, decisions and sometimes stupidity. When I was on 826 Squadron, I nearly conjured the ultimate UAS of getting thrown out of the navy. We were on an attachment with the Dutch Navy, and our ship was moored in Malaga in Spain. One of the Dutch ships was having a cocktail party and along with some others, I was 'volunteered' to represent the Royal Navy.

We threw ourselves into it with enthusiasm, sparkling with polite chit-chat and charm as we graciously accepted liberal top-ups of our drinks and grinned our way through the evening. Meandering back to our ship at the end of the night, my mate Andy Skinner's eyes lit up when he spotted a digger parked on the quay. Being a farmer's lad, he reckoned he knew how to drive it and suggested it could speed up our journey. 'Skins', as he was known, was certain the keys would be kept under the driver's sun visor, so he had a quick fish around and sure enough, there they were.

He fired up the engine and the machine came alive with an eager rumble. Skins sat in the driver's seat, revving the engine, flashing the lights and beeping the horn. Parp, parp! Giggling, I grabbed the lever that operated the small digger arm at the back. Up a bit, down, left a bit, hold it there.

Lovely. We didn't drive it around, but we had a good laugh before eventually deciding it was time to get back to the ship, negative digger. We left it parked up as we found it and climbed onboard to crash in our pits in the bowels of the ship.

My discombobulated brain quickly shut down, but at some stage, I was aware of some words penetrating the haze.

"Hickson... Skinner".

Actually, they might be shouting. They grew louder with each rendition until I was wide awake and staring at the red-faced duty officer standing in our cramped cabin screaming at the pair of us, me in the bottom bunk, Skins above me.

"What do you know about a damaged digger? Get out of those stinking pits, NOW. The Spanish police would like a word."

Oh dear. This does not sound good. I vaguely remember the digger. Did we damage it? My head is throbbing like the inside of a bass drum and my mouth is parched like a desert.

Couldn't I just pop down later? We hustled into our smartest uniforms in double-quick time, the adrenaline surge of panic and dawning realisation doing a decent job of clearing the fog.

The police office was like a scene from a 1970s TV cop caper, with clouds of cigar smoke hanging in the air as Spanish policemen with big moustaches jabbered and pointed fingers at us. It was clear we weren't getting out of this quickly. Eventually, we got a call from a Naval captain stationed in Madrid, the Spanish Naval attaché. He told us the police were going to take us to court that afternoon and he recommended we accept any fine they give us.

Our ship was leaving that night, and he said if we weren't back onboard when it left, he would no longer be able to contain the incident at his level. He couldn't say for sure what would happen to our careers.

Turning up at court, there was some brief hilarity with the officials who thought that as respectable, smart-looking Naval officers we were there to represent some sozzled sailors from the ship's company rather than being the defendants ourselves. We immediately pleaded guilty and accepted the fine, which was way more than we had with us, so we had to call the ship and ask for some cash. We were in a pickle, but they opened the safe and rushed the money over to hand to the digger's owners. Free to go, we rushed back to the ship and sailed safely out of Malaga that night, chastened and sheepish, but still in the Royal Navy, negative a wad of cash.

Our hi-jinks had caused a UDS (undesirable digger state) and nearly cost us our place in the Royal Navy. The serious life lesson and valuable educational takeaway is: don't borrow diggers when you're on a run ashore (Navy slang for a night out). As an aside, very sadly, Andy Skinner died a short while after this incident when his Sea King helicopter crashed into the sea at night after taking off from a ship. A sad loss of a great friend and talented aviator.

So far in this chapter we have been looking at making mistakes due to your own doing. We both want to be clear; no one should get near a vehicle or operate any machinery when under the influence of anything. To give the 'dumper truck' story some context it was 40 years ago, not on a public road but in a private compound.

I faced a dilemma. I had signed up with the Royal Navy for 16 years and my time was up. The natural route was to join the airlines and fly commercially. I'd done my qualifications in preparation, but now the time had come I didn't really want to leave.

Why would I want to leave the Royal Navy? After all, it had given me the chance to do something meaningful, fulfilling, exciting, worthwhile even. By now, I was flying my beloved Hawk almost every day and I also had the distinct privilege of being responsible for parts of the Royal Navy Historic Flight, what's now called Navy Wings. That meant I got to fly and display the Fairey Swordfish, a venerable old biplane which in its World War Two heyday carried a torpedo to attack ships. It scored some big successes too, including sinking a battleship and damaging others at the Battle of Taranto and playing a key part in the sinking of the formidable German battleship Bismarck.

One day news filtered down to us that a Spitfire would be landing at RNAS Yeovilton and as the Historic Flight we would be hosting. It was like being a kid on Christmas Eve. I couldn't wait to get a close look at the plane that fought so spectacularly against the Luftwaffe in the Battle of Britain and helped to secure our skies and bring an end to the war. Even better news for us, the rumour was that the pilot would take one of us flying in his backseat.

The trouble was, there were two of us available and both of us were desperate for the golden ticket. It was either Chris Greaves or me. Over lunch we put forward our case, almost imploring the other to relent. I could think of nothing else I wanted to do more in the world at that precise moment in time, but I knew that Chris had often helped me in my career.

I also sensed it would mean more to him than me despite my longing to go. It was a hard thing to do but I knew it was the right thing to do.

"It's yours Chris, you take the flight," I said.

He looked at me for a brief second, as if computing the permutations and trying to work out what my strategy was but he quickly broke into a huge grin.

“Well, if you’re okay with that... cheers mate, thanks a lot.”

A stunning cobalt sky greeted us the following day and after lunch I pottered out onto the airfield as Chris and the pilot went about various checks before firing up that distinctive twelve-cylinder Rolls-Royce Merlin engine. Its throaty, throbbing roar is so distinctive, emanating power, pride, courage and defiance, the sound of freedom. It was like squeezing down a wormhole back to the 1940s and I looked up, imagining spitfires tumbling around the sky in a dance to the death with their German counterparts. After Chris had taken off, I headed back to my office, forlorn both at the lost chance and the pile of paperwork that greeted me.

A while later I was beavering away at something when I heard the station tannoy announce, “Hickson to Historic Flight, Hickson to Historic Flight... at the rush!”

It wasn’t a normal sign off to one of these calls, so I sprung from my desk and scuttled out to the team’s area on the airfield. When I got there, Greavesy was grinning beside the Spitfire with its pilot, Norman Lees. Norman said Chris had told him the story of how I had offered up the flight and decided I deserved a ride too. He just had time before he had to leave if I could be ready now.

Mentally, I was ready way before then, but I said yes and legged it back to the office to grab my gear. I climbed into my flying suit as fast as I could, cursing myself for sticking my foot where the arm should go in my mad dash to be ready. I grabbed a helmet and ran back outside to meet Norman for a briefing. When he said we were ready to go I skipped up the steps and lowered myself into the back seat, strapping myself in and clocking the pristine gauges and switches, which had been lovingly restored, on the small control panel in front of me.

A member of the ground crew slid the canopy over my head, and I peered out from my glass cocoon as Norman fired up the thunderous engine. Looking past Norman's head and up the long nose of the Spitfire beyond, I watched the four blades of the propeller gather pace before rotating into the faint blur of a circle. This is it, old chum, the holy grail. You're actually going up in a Spitfire.

Take it all in, absorb it, watch in super high definition so it never fades in your mind.

Norman taxied out to the runway and once ready, eased off the brakes and built the speed gently until we roared down the tarmac and lifted into the Somerset sky. The Spitfire requires knowledge to fly so there was no way I could just jump in, grab the controls and take off. But once we were airborne, Norman handed her over to me. As I held the control column gently in my right hand, I wondered how many vigorous young men had clambered into this aircraft back in the day, literally to go and fight for their lives.

I held her straight and level for a while, just savouring the low rumble of the Rolls-Royce engine, waggling the wings now and then to feel the taught response of the controls. Norman suggested we head south towards Yeovil, so I moved my hand over to the left to bank around, putting the Spitfire on her wing end as I gazed down through the canopy at the patchwork of green fields below. Happy I knew what I was doing, Norman asked if I wanted to fly a victory roll. I really did.

I eased the nose up to about forty-five degrees to the left and rocked the control column over, allowing her to roll lazily over onto her back before continuing round to finish the right way up. That felt bloody good. It was the signature move of the wartime flying aces to celebrate a successful mission. I felt privileged enough to be sitting in the aircraft, let alone flying it, but to perform a victory roll made me feel like my flying career was complete.

After twenty magical minutes our time was up, and Norman took over the controls to land back at Yeovilton. I couldn't stop smiling and Chris and I talked of nothing but our flights for the rest of the day.

That flight will stay with me forever. Tragically, a week later, Norman and his passenger died when the same Spitfire crashed at Goodwood airfield. It was a brutal reminder of how thin the line is between privilege and loss.

So, leaving the navy was a tough decision. I could have signed up for longer. I was very happy and enjoyed the rhythm of bobbing along from one job to another. I knew I was only going sideways in the navy and I was okay with that.

I wasn't interested in the quest to clamber up the promotion ladder, but I also knew that deep down in my core I had a desire for real change, like a magnet pulling me inexorably towards the door. It was going to be now or never to join the airlines. Even so, I spent the months approaching the end agonising and wrestling with the dilemma.

I would make a concrete decision one minute and then do a complete mental U-turn in the time it took me to walk from my front door to the garden gate. Eventually it was time to make a decision, so I left the best job in the world. My world, anyway. To smooth my torment, I joined the Royal Navy Reserves and was able to go back and fly the Hawk whenever I wanted to.

I secured a job as a first officer with GB Airways on the Airbus A320 and spent six weeks at Airbus HQ in

Toulouse in France getting up to speed. My second career as a commercial airline pilot had begun. The first mistake I made joining the commercial sector was assuming that because I was a military pilot that made me a better aviator. I got that monumentally wrong.

Most commercial pilots are superb, highly motivated and very talented, they just possess some different skill sets to military aviators. It took me a while to recognise that, but it was clear when I watched them operate the aircraft. They were professionals, accurate with their flying, polished with their management of tasks and just great aviators to be around. I suspect it's a trait with many people moving jobs in civvie street and thinking the perceived cachet of one organisation puts them on a pedestal, whereas the truth is there are highly skilled people everywhere.

The minute you think you're the kingpin and have nothing to learn is the beginning of your downfall, which is worth bearing in mind when switching jobs and jumping on and off escalators.

The Airbus was very modern for its time with outstanding capabilities. It is fly-by-wire, which means its flight control computers analyse the pilot's input and use electronic signals to produce the required outcome. Crucially, the system knows how the aircraft should perform and won't allow certain outcomes to occur, such as stalling when the angle of attack of the wing becomes too great to produce lift. At this point it would intervene and give you more thrust.

As such, the A320 is a smart aircraft, and it prevents the pilot operating outside its safe performance envelope. You do need to understand it though, otherwise you'll spend plenty of time wondering what the hell it is up to. I progressed to captain after a couple of years and relished the responsibility, leadership and decision-making that came with the role. Understanding people's behaviours had always fascinated me and the more situations I encountered flying on the line, the more I was driven to discover more.

After all, for all the Airbus' wizardry, it is still flown by human beings with their inherent frailties and biases. To stay fresh and keep moving forward, I did a human factors training course and took on a role as the CRM manager with the airline alongside my usual flying schedule.

Even though I was an airline captain and CRM trainer, I wasn't immune to biases of my own. Confirmation bias is the brain's natural tendency to interpret new evidence as confirmation of one's existing beliefs or theories. The brain wants to take the path of least resistance and make the easier decisions. One example of this led me to lose thousands of pounds in a bank scam.

This was before scams were part of our everyday language.

One day Mandy texted me to say our bank was going to call me to discuss some unusual activity on one of our accounts. She was busy at work so couldn't chat. Sure enough, not long after that my phone rang and the number said it was the bank. So far, so good.

No alarm bells. I spoke to a very charming, very helpful lady who said they were investigating this unusual activity. She asked some general questions such as whether I had done any online shopping recently, or paid for something small using the app. Yes, I said, I bought something in the gym yesterday.

This went on for a while and then she asked for four random digits from my customer reference number. She asked some more questions and then said she could see that

£40,000 had been moved out of our savings account into two of our other accounts. Did I make these transfers, she asked? No. So now it looked like someone had accessed our account.

Then she asked if we had added another telephone number. Again, no. It was very compelling and she was working hard to help us resolve this. She said we needed to freeze the accounts immediately.

I was very grateful and thanked her. I watched live on the screen in front of me as the accounts all changed to 'Inactive'. She said to be safe, until we could reactivate them the following day, we needed to move the money to a holding account. Yes, sounds sensible, I said. Thanks very much.

I grabbed my card reader and made the payments to the account she gave me, once for the personal account and once for the business account, both at the £20,000 transfer limit for the day.

"This must be very distressing for you, but don't worry, we'll get it sorted," she said.

I thanked her profusely again, but I did have a nagging doubt. "How do I know this isn't a scam?"

Smoothly, she replied that the phone number that first came up said it was from my bank and told me to cross reference the number she was calling from with the bank's number on the back of my credit card. All seemed fair enough. She said she would ring back tomorrow to set up the accounts, so I thanked her again, relieved to have got it sorted. Phew.

Could have been a bit of a nightmare, that. But when I spoke to Mandy later that night, she said the accounts didn't look frozen and there was £40,000 missing. The penny dropped. The supposed bank lady had been a scammer, manipulating our accounts as I looked on, changing the name on the account to say 'Inactive' to make me think it was frozen.

A sense of dread spread over me like a cold blanket, and I felt sick. It was like the rest of the world was looking at me, pointing and laughing and calling me an idiot. I was no longer Craig the airline captain, I was Craig the five-year-old, feeling small and stupid. I'd been the victim of a very clever, very patient push-pull scam.

It took more than eighteen months of wrangling with the bank, a complaint to the Financial Ombudsman and bucketloads of stress before the money was refunded. The point is, despite some red flags in hindsight, my cognitive bias was that I wanted to believe the lady on the phone was there to help. I'm all about helping others and naively thought so are other people. I couldn't believe that such evil morons could do that to someone.

In the context of human errors and bias, it is an example of the brain filling in the gaps without challenging the system. Mandy's initial call had primed me. I did briefly challenge it, but not robustly enough, too quick to revert to the norm and assume it was all alright. That's why aviation, through CRM training, strives to build in checks to the process to prevent errors and biases slipping through.

The fundamental point is that we all make mistakes in life and acknowledging that is half the battle. The flex is to not dwell on them, learn from them and provide feedback where relevant, so others don't make the same mistakes. An enlightened leadership will ask whether more training is needed, are the correct systems in place, could they help more? Human error remains a significant threat and managing it needs robustness and resilience from both the individual and the company. Approaching it on a higher plane, rather than just playing the blame game, will stand you in good stead on your path.

I took off from London Heathrow bound for Marrakech in Morocco via Casablanca. It was a route I flew regularly, and I knew most of the crew onboard pretty well, some were friends. As routine as a trip could be, this was up there. The leg down to Casablanca passed without incident and then we did the short hop to Marrakech, its sand-coloured old city gradually showing itself from the desert, with the snow-dusted Atlas Mountains off in the distance.

As a captain it had been a very low demand kind of day and I was feeling peaceful and happy, watching the setting sun cast a golden glow as we approached. As I brought the aircraft onto the stand, I noticed I'd received a message on the ACARS system, like a text message service from the airline, asking me to call home. The words themselves were innocuous, but I sensed they masked something much bigger, like walking through the gate of a haunted house. You wouldn't normally get a message like this for mundane reasons, such as asking you to pick up a pint of milk on your way home.

My thoughts darted down all sorts of dark passages and dead ends. Perhaps it was something to do with my elderly parents. I knew I had to find a quiet spot to make the call so once the passengers had disembarked and I'd shut down the jet, I nipped from the cockpit to call home from the end of the jetty. Mandy picked up the phone, but it was difficult to understand her because she was sobbing.

"Craig, I can't believe it..."

"Believe what?"

There was a pause. "I'm so sorry darling, but Paul has died."

"Er, what, my brother Paul. No, are you sure, how, that's ridiculous, he can't, wait, what...?"

My thoughts and emotions had been put into a mixer, firing out words scattergun. When I came to a stop, Mandy gathered herself.

"All we know for now is he's been found dead in a hotel in Pakistan. Craigy, I'm so sorry."

"But Paul... no, can't be, he's a fit, healthy guy... "

My heart hammered like a speeding tube train and I was staring, shaking my head, agitated like a panicked and cornered animal. I just couldn't take it in. It was too big, too overwhelming, too heartbreaking. It just couldn't be real.

Not him. Not now. Not ever. My eyes burned and then filled with tears.

It was impossible to stop the flood.

After the navy, Paul went to university and studied for a degree, then did a masters and got a job in IT with a bank in Australia. He and his girlfriend were on holiday in Sri Lanka when the Boxing Day Tsunami hit in 2004. He'd phoned me up at 6am and asked how I was. I said I was fine, bit of a headache but given the amount I'd drunk the day before, not so bad.

He said he was alive, which I thought to be an odd comment and told me to put the TV on. Still in a Christmas fug, the enormity of the disaster hit me like a dumper truck. Paul had been lucky, he had been sitting on the balcony of his hotel room and had seen the tsunami approaching. He saw bodies from the swimming pool in front of the hotel being smashed into the side of the building below, but due to staying on a higher floor he was safe.

The scale of the disaster affected him deeply and he stayed out in Sri Lanka to help the relief effort. It gave him a sort of life epiphany too. He thought he was wasting time in computing and decided there were bigger things in the world. He eventually switched careers and landed a job with the United Nations.

On October 8, 2005 Pakistan suffered a devastating earthquake in the Kashmir region. The official death toll was about 88,000, but some estimates say it could have been far more. Paul had been deployed to Pakistan to help with the relief effort and had been put in charge of clearing all the rubble from the destroyed sites so that building work could begin. During a weekend off in Islamabad he had failed to turn up in the lobby to meet some colleagues.

Now he'd been found dead in his hotel room. The official cause of death from the UK was that he died of a heroin overdose, a death due to misadventure, that wasn't the Paul I knew. The Pakistan authorities found no toxins in his body and stated on his death certificate that he had died of natural causes. These two conflicting conclusions have always troubled me, I doubt I will ever totally understand the reasons behind his death.

I half stumbled back to the aircraft, as if the 'walk' signals from my brain to my legs were being blocked. I gathered myself enough to tell the crew very briefly that I'd received some bad news and said I was just going to go to the hotel. As a captain I was treated like royalty and had a top-floor suite to myself, but it meant nothing. I just lay on the bed, sobbing and fighting demons.

Paul, no, not you... I just want to see you again, talk to

you. Please, God… why? Make this nightmare stop…

Sleeping was out of the question. I played all sorts of scenarios out in my head, about how and why he had died, about our young lives together, about what now.

My alarm roused me from whatever delirious, fevered half-sleep I'd managed. I dragged myself out of bed for a shower and shave. Looking at myself in the mirror I appeared like the undead, ghostly white with dark, sunken, red-rimmed eyes. Panic rose at the thought of having to captain an aircraft back to the UK.

I made it downstairs to get the transport to the airport and was met by some shocked faces at my haggard appearance. By now the crew knew what had happened to Paul. I told them that I would be fine to fly back and wanted very much to do the trip. They said that's fine Craig, whatever you want to do.

They knew me, I knew them, and everyone seemed to think it was a reasonable idea. But, of course, safety is number one priority and looking back, was I really safe to fly? You would have to say that my judgment was unbelievably poor. I wasn't in a fit state to fly and should have held up my hands. On an A320 there are two pilots – the pilot flying (PF) and the pilot monitoring (PM).

My first officer was very experienced, in fact he was older than me, and he said he would fly the aircraft and make all the operational decisions such as how much fuel to carry. I could just monitor the weather and man the radios. It seemed like a good plan.

When you fuel up a commercial airliner you normally work out the total amount of fuel required, which includes a final reserve of 30 minutes' worth of flying time on top of enough fuel should you need to make a diversion. In our case we would probably divert from Heathrow to Gatwick should a problem arise. I went through my duties in a perfunctory way, getting the job done but not quite present.

We took off for Casablanca where we picked up some more passengers and then set off back to London.

When we were cruising, I was just staring vacantly out of the window, my mind still swirling like a violent snowstorm. I'd occasionally flick my eyes to the instruments just to check – I was still the captain of the aircraft – but then I noticed we were going to be overweight to land; in other words, we had too much fuel on board. You can't land overweight unless it's an emergency because of structural limits to the undercarriage. You can't just chance it and think you will be alright; you must do something about it.

Now we had a real threat to manage and I had to switch on. One way of burning more fuel is to fly lower because the air is thicker and so the engines have to work harder. I got on the radio to Paris air traffic control to request an early descent, about 300 miles out from Heathrow. Putting down the landing gear is another way to burn fuel as it creates more drag, so we did that about 40 miles from Heathrow.

We also increased our speed to eat through some more fuel, but then this adds to the already complicated workload of air traffic control who had to ask other aircraft approaching Heathrow to slow down. We trapped and mitigated the threat and got down safely but the mistake of taking too much fuel created a substantial workload for us, air traffic control and other aircraft and made a routine flight into a stressful flight.

But the real human error is that I should not have put the first officer in that position in the first place by insisting I fly home in the poor state I was in. Looking back, both personally and professionally, I've tried to analyse why I was unable to make the right decision. I knew in my mind I wasn't right and on a normal day you'd phone up and say I'm not fit to fly. The answer probably lies in the fact my motivation was completely wrong; it was about returning home as quickly as I could to be with Mandy and my parents, to process Paul's death.

This story also highlights a fundamental culture issue. One look at my face after crying all night and not sleeping might have given the signal to start asking questions. This is not in any way blaming individuals, but it does beg the question, was the system, the CRM, the Golden Five, all of that human factors stuff, robust enough to deal with a latent threat such as this?

I wouldn't say we put anyone in any danger that day, but we definitely made some mistakes. There are times in life when you can't do it all by yourself and in hindsight, the system should have saved me from myself. Of course, questioning the captain is difficult for some people and goes back to the environment that has been created and the human factors training. But maybe the airline could have done more, at least checking in after sending the ACARS, which is unusual.

Is everything okay, do we need to get someone to cover you? I understand the brain wants to take the path of least resistance. It is easier for us to just fly home, to believe it was the bank calling. It's natural, but does it make it right? I don't think so. So when you get this nagging feeling that all is not well, sit up and pay attention and don't always take the easier path.

I still think of Paul every day and I talk about him a lot to family and friends. He made a big impact on me when he was around, but bizarrely, he has made an even bigger impact since his death. There is no question that I live my life in the now because of what happened to him. There is no five-year plan, just a 'let's get on with it' attitude.

Grab all the fun, adventure and experiences you can with the people who are most important to you.

CHAPTER 7

YOUR CAPTAIN SPEAKING

MANDY: Put me in any environment, and I feel an almost irresistible urge to take charge, to lead, to be the one pulling the strings. It's as if I've been under a lifelong spell, like some character from Harry Potter. Someone must have waved a wand over my cot and muttered 'Bossio', dooming me to a lifetime of charging ahead, trying to take control. I'm sure to some people it's a tad annoying.

Ironically, you could argue I'm not actually in control of myself, just compulsively trying to lead without looking at the bigger picture. But what does it even mean to be a leader? Countless books, seminars and TED Talks dissect leadership in excruciating detail, delivered by people with great hair, dazzling teeth and a lot more PowerPoint slides than I'll ever need.

Personality models like Myers-Briggs and Insights promise to unlock our leadership potential, mapping out whether we're natural-born commanders or better suited to staying in the pack. You will find examples of leadership throughout this book. But rather than a 'How to lead' chapter, this is more of a personal reflection on what leadership really is.

Interestingly, I've never really had a job in a position of leadership. Or should I say a job title that infers leadership. The military recruits its officers on leadership potential and spends plenty of time and money honing that. But as a pilot in the RAF, I was just flying my own Tornado around, much like you drive your car, albeit faster, sometimes upside down and with more live weapons.

Yes, I had a navigator sitting behind me, but we were a team. It's true that on occasion I would lead a mission, making the calls for a formation of jets, say, on a bombing run behind enemy lines. When that missile locked on to me in Iraq, I was the leader of four Tornados on patrol policing the no-fly zone. The squadron boss was flying alongside me in the four-ship, but I was the designated leader that night.

After we evaded the missile, I had some decisions to make while Jacko, my navigator, plotted a course to rejoin the other three jets. We had clearly been subjected to an aggressive act by the enemy, so we were now within our rights to attack a designated target we had been pre-assigned before the mission. It was my job to contact the mission commander flying high over the Persian Gulf to get authorisation to attack.

"Warrior, this is Spartan One. We've been locked-on by a SAM (surface-to-air missile). Permission to engage targets."

"Roger that, Spartan One, stand by," replied a clipped voice from somewhere in the heavens above.

I glanced down at the fuel gauge and realised we had another problem. The evasion manoeuvre had cost us precious gas and the needle was approaching the red zone. I blinked hard a couple of times just to check I was seeing it right. Flipping heck, we're low.

We might just have enough to attack and get back if it all went swimmingly, but the weather was deteriorating at base and we wouldn't have enough fuel to divert somewhere else if it dropped below minimums. We could go and hook up with a tanker circling above Saudi Arabia first, but there were scores of allied aircraft up and about that night and any queuing behind the tanker could prove critical. Blimey, this is hard. What to do? A few moments later the radio sprung into life.

"Spartan One, you are free to engage targets."

Right then, Mands, action time.

I got on the radio and assigned each member of the team a task. Jacko's job was to find the target. I asked the boss flying as number two to plot a route to the tanker, number three was to work on a course and timings from the tanker to the target and how much fuel we'd need to prosecute the attack. I asked number four to get a detailed weather report, so we had covered all our bases.

This wasn't me being proactive and quick thinking, this was protocol we had practised over and over again. We flew on in silence for a few minutes, save for the thump of my heart thudding against the G-suit and the jet's low chrrr, oblivious to the human drama of its inhabitants. When everyone came back on the radio, we pooled our thoughts and I made the call. Gentlemen, let's go and find that tanker.

The fact that at no point did the boss step in, is a great example of leaders trusting and empowering their team. The whole situation highlights the attitude that leadership is an action not a title. So, I had a sort of title in that I had been made leader that night, rather than just barging in and taking control, but I was a junior pilot by rank and experience and it would have been easy for someone more senior to take over. But this would have been demoralising, suggesting I didn't have the capacity or experience to do the job.

My lack of official leadership title in the RAF was mainly down to circumstance. Because I had children and I took a job behind the front line, I was told that I would never be promoted because I was no longer following the traditional career pathway that had worked for my male counterparts for so many years. They had obviously changed the policy to allow women to become pilots in the RAF but hadn't really thought through all the permutations of how becoming a parent might impact their careers. When I was due to return to work following maternity leave after my second son was born, I was told I was being posted to a Tornado GR4 squadron and would be deploying to Afghanistan.

I felt it might be rather difficult to breastfeed my four-month-old baby from overseas, so I did my research and found a job elsewhere in the RAF that would suit my situation much better. I therefore remained at the rank of Flight Lieutenant and never became Squadron Leader, Wing Commander or Group Captain, roles that conjure up images of square-shouldered heroes who have risen above the crowd to act as a focal point and an inspiration for others. It nags at me, because as someone who had always been told I was a 'natural leader' I've always felt as if I didn't achieve what I should have, I didn't fulfil my potential. This feeling of regret was worse when I first left the RAF, but it has faded with age, mainly because my thinking around leadership has changed, both what it is and what it represents.

A while back I was offered the chance to apply to become an honorary Group Captain with 601 Squadron, a panel of advisers external to the Royal Air Force who act as a sounding board to the chiefs of the air staff. I was very flattered to have been considered. As well as being a fascinating role it would have scratched my itch to say I had moved up the ladder. And by three ranks as well, equivalent to a colonel in the army or a captain in the navy.

Quite the promotion then. But talking to Craig (who is so frustratingly nearly always right) I realised I was thinking of doing it for all the wrong reasons. I wanted to wear a uniform with more stripes on it. As a very wise friend, Paul Gilbert, nicely surmises in his book *The Compassionate Mind,* I was being a tenant of my past and not an architect of my future.

Reasonably reluctantly, I removed my application.

I was then contacted out of the blue by a truly inspirational leader, Air Marshal Philip Osborn (or Osby to his friends). He had been the boss of 13 Squadron when I was serving on II(AC) squadron. I had always got on well with him and I loved his leadership style. I'd seen how his emotional intelligence and people-first leadership set him apart.

He had a rare ability to make everyone feel valued, he empowered individuals to take ownership and created a culture of trust, even in the highest-pressure environments, proving that great leadership is as much about understanding people as it is about strategy. I also loved his sense of humour. He asked whether I would consider joining the RAF Charitable Trust as a trustee. From shaping the Trust's strategy to engaging with air cadets, aviation scholars and the wider RAF family, it was an opportunity to influence the future of aviation while staying connected to the values and teamwork that defined my own career.

Plus, being part of events like the Royal International Air Tattoo (RIAT) would keep my love for aviation alive in the most exhilarating way. This was exactly what I had been waiting for. This was a role I would be taking for the right reasons.

In my career as a speaker, I'm clearly not leading anyone. Or am I? Because I've come to realise leadership isn't just about rank, authority or command – it's about influence. When I stand on a stage, especially in front of young people in schools, I realise that I am leading in a different way. My words and my experiences all have the power to inspire, challenge and shape perspectives.

I might not be issuing orders or making life-and-death decisions like I once did in the cockpit, but I am guiding people – helping them see what's possible when they back themselves, take risks and step beyond their comfort zones. Thought leadership and projecting a positive image on social media is an extension of that. That's why I took to LinkedIn to challenge President Trump's claim that diversity hiring policies led to the tragic airline crash in Washington, DC in January 2025. I was furious.

Aviation safety has never been about politics; it's about precision, training and excellence. My post, calling for focus on facts over rhetoric, sparked more comments and reactions than I'd ever seen before.

My thinking on leadership has evolved. There is the traditional path of climbing the ladder, taking on more responsibility and leading teams, either at work or in other activities; there is leading by influence; and there is personal leadership, where you take the initiative and take action even though your title might not suggest you are a 'leader'. Sometimes, the most powerful thing you can do as a leader is simply speaking up.

One question I get asked a lot is: "What advice would you give to your twenty-year-old self?" My answer, one of my absolute mantras, is simple: be unapologetically you. After all, the world doesn't need more people blending in. We all radiate and shine in our own way and we should recognise that. The same goes for leadership; put yourself forward, learn the skills but do it your way.

Increasingly, people don't want distant, untouchable figures, they want authenticity, honesty and vulnerability. And for women in leadership, it's no longer about mimicking male counterparts. Diversity isn't a weakness, it's an asset. True leadership comes from embracing who you are and bringing that to the table.

It's about using your voice.

We were out in Nevada in the US, flying out of Nellis Air Force Base during Red Flag, a huge multinational air combat exercise where the jets are loud, the tempo is high, and the nights are long. One evening, the whole squadron was heading out for dinner and I decided to make an effort. A dress, a bit of lipstick, heels that weren't standard issue – nothing outrageous, but certainly not my usual flying suit and boots.

I walked into the foyer of the hotel where we were all meeting. Michel, a smooth French exchange navigator, turned towards me, smiled and said, "Mandy, you look beautiful this evening."

Before I could even react, Richard, standing next to him, burst out laughing, playfully smacked Michel on the head and said, "You can't say that to Mandy, she's one of the boys." Michel shrugged and responded with the kind of weary elegance only a Frenchman can pull off: "Puh. You Brits have so much to learn about women." It made everyone laugh, and on the surface, it was a throwaway moment. But for me, it was anything but.

The truth was, I had become one of the boys. I'd spent so long trying to fit in, mirroring the banter, the behaviour, even the blazer-and-chinos uniform when we travelled, that I'd gradually erased the parts of myself that didn't align with the squadron mould. It had worked in the sense that I was just considered one of the team, even though I was a woman. But there's a massive difference between fitting in and belonging.

Fitting in meant modifying myself to be accepted. Belonging meant being accepted as myself.

That moment with Michel was a spark. It made me realise I had been burying my own authenticity. I quietly resolved to be more me, more Mandy and less man! It may have been only subtle but when I changed, I sensed the atmosphere began to change too. There was possibly a bit less posturing, people hiding behind masks and slightly more honesty and real conversations.

What began as a comment about a dress turned into a quiet revolution in culture. And it reminded me that the strongest teams aren't built on conformity. They're built on trust, respect and a shared sense of belonging, where who you are is enough.

One of the best leaders I know is one of my closest friends, Lynette Jackson, who I met on the very first day at the University of Birmingham. Since those fun-filled times she has held several senior communications roles in some leading companies and her style mirrors everything I admire about authentic leadership. She leads with a rare blend of strategic clarity and human empathy. She believes that true leadership isn't about commanding a room, it's about creating spaces where people feel heard, valued and empowered to act. Lynette's example reminds me that leadership starts with being genuine, listening deeply and aligning people around a clear and inspiring vision.

She reminds me that it's often the smallest things that truly create trust. She remembers her team's birthdays, their children's names, illnesses and life events. She sends cards and ensures that her team feels valued. I've seen Lynette in action, and I've always felt so incredibly inspired by how her team talks to her, respects her and knows that she has their backs.

This is how modern-day leaders should act.

We had just enough fuel to complete the mission and get back. Then the news came through that our assigned tanker had gone unserviceable. A replacement was on its way: an American KC-135.

I'd never refuelled from one before. I gave it a go and missed. I tried again and missed again. At that point, I made the call to pull out and let my boss take the slot.

He refuelled successfully, and we carried on with the mission. But I felt like I'd failed.

Back on the ground, my navigator turned to me and said:

"That was a brilliant call. I pressured you to try again, I just didn't want to miss out. But you were the only one thinking straight."

His words stopped me in my tracks because leadership isn't about being the best at everything. It's about knowing your limits, keeping a cool head under pressure, and making the call that serves the team even if it dents your ego. We were the only crew to hit our target that night. The commander-in-chief confirmed it in the debrief.

And I came away from that flight with more insight than I'd learned in years: Leadership means staying clear-headed when it counts.

It's knowing when to step aside so someone else can succeed.

It's about building the kind of team where everyone's voice and judgment matters. That was the moment I truly understood psychological safety.

Nowadays I talk a lot about psychological safety and for good reason. It's not just a buzzword. Psychological safety is what allows people to take interpersonal risks without fear of judgment, rejection or punishment. It's what gives someone the courage to say, "I don't know" or "I messed up" or "I've got a different view" without worrying they'll be laughed at, undermined or ignored.

That's crucial, because in high-stakes environments, whether it's flying a jet at 500 knots or managing a tough client negotiation, you need the truth from your team. Not what they think you want to hear.

CRAIG: We are surrounded by this word leadership; is it the ultimate destination, that only by achieving this superpower will we be successful? I am not so sure this is the right measure of success. I am not a natural leader. I can step up if I think I really need to, but if there is someone equally as capable but much more eager, I don't feel the need to thrust myself forward.

As someone who tends more towards the introvert end of the spectrum – although I certainly have my extrovert moments, like many people – this striving for leadership is not a natural place for me. Whereas Mandy might walk straight into it, I would give it some thought and recognise I might need to up my game to achieve the same outcome. But when the time is right, I think I am able to motivate, assimilate information and use this to make good decisions and communicate effectively.

But leadership is a subjective topic. One person's idea of assertive, confident, initiative-taking leadership might be another's idea of pushy, annoying, overbearing attention-seeker. Who is to say who is right? To me, there are times to lead and times to let others lead. There is no single blueprint to being a leader, it comes in all shapes and sizes.

Leadership can also be nurtured, often bringing out the innate leader in all of us. I disagree with the notion that a leader always has to be an extrovert, a look-at-me thruster. Introverts can make very effective leaders in the right situation. What I am clear about is that all leaders need to display similar behaviours: encouraging of team participation and open communication; demonstrating initiative and providing direction when required; engaging others in planning; considering input from others; addressing and resolving conflict and disagreements in a positive way; being decisive when required; accepting responsibility.

I accept if you are leading a four-ship of Tornados over the border there is a requirement to show 'leadership skills'. But leadership in that environment wasn't about barking orders or having the most experience, it was about trust, communication and ensuring the entire team operated as a single unit. That mission wasn't successful because one person was an exceptional leader; it worked because everyone had trained relentlessly, understood their roles and all knew how to work together. Someone had to oversee making the final call, yes, but leadership was shared amongst all.

If you were asked who the leader is on a commercial airline you might quite reasonably suggest it is the captain. Certainly, they have the authority because of their position. Are they good leaders? Hopefully yes, but maybe not. What about the cabin crew? Do they need these qualities? Definitely.

There's a massive misperception that as the captain, I'm the leader. I am certainly responsible for the safety of the people on board and pointing the aircraft in the right direction, but in the airlines, you need the most junior member in the aircraft to be able to show extraordinary leadership skills. Look at the accident in Toronto in February 2025 when a passenger jet operated by Delta Airline flipped over on landing and burst into flames. All 76 passengers and four crew survived.

The passengers described their amazement after most of them escaped unscathed from an aircraft that was upside down. Undoubtedly, the cabin crew played a huge and significant part in this successful outcome. Had they trained for this exact scenario? I doubt it. What they did display was their ability to remain composed and motivate all the passengers to get out of the aircraft in a safe way despite the inevitable stress and fear they would be exposed to.

To me, this is true leadership.

From all my various jobs over the years, several people stand out for different reasons when discussing leadership. One was a squadron boss, who I felt uncomfortable to be around. I would be anxious looking at the flying programme for the next day to see if I had been put down to fly with him. Because of his reputation I would feel under confident. He was a senior officer.

I honestly thought each flight with him could be my last. Even though I'd got through all that training and passed test after test to reach the front line, I wouldn't sleep the night before, fretting and lying in turmoil, going back over my flying profiles to make sure I didn't slip up. In briefings he would be challenging, confrontational if you like, firing out technical questions based on some in-depth system knowledge, such as what does the ramp generator do in the radio altimeter system? He seemed to enjoy uncovering a weakness and an opportunity for him to pass on his superior knowledge and experience. You could argue this hard-nosed attitude was achieving the results we needed, keeping people on their toes, guarding against complacency, but I don't see it that way.

I don't believe you can drive people by fear and expect to get a good result. I will say, though, that he was exceptional when the squadron lost an aircraft and two aircrew were killed. We were all devastated and the boss brought the squadron together and managed to keep it focused on our front-line commitments while allowing us to grieve. He was outstanding with all the families too.

So, he was a very good situational leader and sharp on crisis management. But there's a big difference between being a situational leader and an everyday leader. We often glamourise crisis leadership because it looks more dramatic. These leaders are brilliant when the heat is on.

They can make fast decisions, hold their nerve and rally teams through chaos. I've worked with plenty like that in the cockpit, who were calm in the face of engine failure and decisive in high-pressure missions. They're the person you want when everything's going wrong.

Winston Churchill with his rousing wartime speeches is a good example, lifting the nation's morale and tackling the dark threat of Nazism head on. But he wasn't quite so impressive in peacetime, losing the 1945 general election just months after leading Britain to victory. That's because the skills needed to inspire a nation during war; stirring rhetoric, bold vision, and focus on a single threat - don't always translate into the collaborative, emotionally intelligent leadership required to navigate everyday politics. But everyday leadership is where real culture is built.

It's not about a single moment, it's about consistency. It's leading when no one's watching. It's turning up, supporting your team, spotting the quieter threats like low morale or creeping disengagement and dealing with them before they escalate. It's saying, "Are you okay?" at the right moment and really meaning it.

Everyday leaders might never make the history books, but they shape everything from trust to performance to wellbeing. The best leaders know when to be which. They can rise to the moment when needed and then switch gears, listen, support and empower when things are ticking along.

Interestingly, that squadron boss and I have followed fairly similar careers after the military and we've had occasion to talk about the old days. There is no question in my mind about his passion for flying. I can see he is actually a very kind and caring person. He agrees with my comments on his leadership style.

He says that's how he was trained as a leader and that's how he thought it had to be done; hit them over the head with a hammer and see how they respond. That's what he thought was right at the time, a style to match his personality. But to me it is an example of a cultural shift and how we need to continually evolve. You may well have had a similar experience with a head teacher or an office colleague who turned out not to be an ogre after all.

Clearly, there are myriad different ways of doing things and styles of leadership, as the textbooks and TED Talks might tell you. There is no cut-and-paste blueprint to being a good leader. It is subjective and what fires one person up might douse the flames of another. The questions I would ask are, "Is your style working? Are you getting the most out of your people?" If not, then perhaps you need to modify your own behaviours to ensure everyone is onboard.

One incredible leader I worked with in my navy days was a guy called Andy Vanes. Interestingly, Andy was not my boss. Within the military's strict hierarchy, 'Vanesy', as everyone knew him, was a chief petty officer aircrewman so he sat below me in the rank structure because he was a non-commissioned officer. But with Vanesy that notion of rank-based leadership was forgotten.

In my opinion he deserves the rank of legend. If I had to go into battle, I would take Vanesy every day. He was a perfect example of someone who exuded personal leadership and radiated positivity, team spirit and a can-do attitude around all those he came into contact with and probably beyond. He was an initiative-taker, a do-er, a fixer, a guy who could anticipate issues and find a way forward, someone his peers rallied around.

I trusted him implicitly. Even though I was the officer I often felt he was leading me, and I'm fine with saying that. We were stationed at RNAS Yeovilton on the Heron Flight and we had a lot of fun flying around Europe in a Jetstream.

Once, flying troops back from Split during the Bosnia conflict we approached Yeovilton on minimum fuel, almost down to the fumes alone. On final approach I pressed the button to put the wheels down for landing, expecting to see three green lights flash up on the panel, indicating the gear was deployed. Instead, I did a full double take as I realised there were only two. That meant in theory that we only had two of the three sets of wheels down and fixed in place.

My eyes widened as my brain quickly computed the issue and tried to fight off the little voices telling me this was a bit of a nightmare. But Vanesy wasn't panicking. He calmly reached down and grabbed the Flight Reference Cards, essentially the instruction manual for when things go wrong, and flicked to the right page.

"Recycle the gear," he said, reading off the checklist like a librarian with one eye on their lunch break.

That meant selecting the up and then down lever to see if that changed anything. Next on the list was to try the back-up system which works by gravity. If that fails you are committed to landing with an abnormal gear extension, meaning you land with the failure which might be without the landing gear down and locked in place. I pushed the landing gear lever back to the retracted position, waited a moment or so then flicked it down to the extended position.

Three greens. Phew. Things are looking up. I could do without an emergency; I've got things to do later.

Must have been a faulty connection somewhere in the electrics. Vanesy looked over at me and winked. While Andy may not have had the stripes of a leader in terms of the rank structure, he was without doubt one of the most effective people I have ever worked with. He displayed all the positive behaviours associated with an aviator at the top of his game.

It goes to show that titles are not everything.

In the airlines, the best boss I ever had, possibly the best leader of my entire career, was the former EasyJet chief executive Dame Carolyn McCall. Before she joined, I would say to people that I worked for an airline. When she took over, I would tell people I worked for EasyJet. I became proud of it because of the impact she had on the business.

She completely turned around this low-cost orange airline into something people were proud to say they worked for. As well as all the business nous, she was a motivator and primarily interested in people.

Once, she came to Gatwick for the opening of a new training centre, which attracted quite a lot of press and travel journalists. I was mooching about on my lunch break and thought I'd pop up to the area on the top floor where they were hosting the event to poke my head in. One thing Carolyn announced was the Amy Johnson scheme to get more women into flying. My ears pricked up at this and I thought I could add some value.

It occurred to me that I could try to introduce myself, but there was a lot of buzz and people milling about after the formalities and Carolyn was constantly in demand. I hung around until the crowd had thinned out and then sensing she was clear, I hit the afterburners and went over. With a big smile I held out my hand and introduced myself and said I was interested in the announcement and could I ask her a bit more about it. She appeared a little defensive at first, as if I was going to cause trouble but I quickly said that my wife Mandy was one of the first female RAF front-line Tornado pilots and that she might be of some use to the scheme.

Carolyn instantly softened and said she had a meeting next door but that I should go with her. I got cold feet and said I would just send her an email, but she insisted. So, I followed her into an adjoining room where there was a buffet lunch laid out. Immediately people swooped towards her, demanding her attention.

I got talking to some other people and thought I'd lost my chance but eventually I caught her gaze over the crowd and she excused herself from her conversation and came straight over.

"Craig, how can I help?"

I explained a bit more about Mandy's story and said that if there were any synergies, or any way for Mandy to get involved she would be more than happy to help. Carolyn was all about empowering women and she said that it was a brilliant idea. She got the process started and Mandy came on board. I thought Carolyn was excellent as a leader because she actively listened and was genuinely interested in her people.

There was no arrogance at all. I would have followed her to the end of the world. People were sad when she decided to leave. It's no surprise to me that the EasyJet share price went up threefold in her time there.

So much is made of leadership being the ultimate destination. You can't move on social media and elsewhere for people spouting off about it as if becoming a leader is the only game in town. I take a far more holistic view. It is one aspect of who I am but what I strive to be is the best version of myself and that includes lots of different aspects.

What is relevant to my path is that I am a good professional aviator, able to fly the plane with all the necessary stick and rudder skills. I also want to be recognised for my ability to communicate with people, to be able to stand up in front of a room of trainees and conduct an engaging session and facilitate a debate and train pilots in groups or as individuals. I'd like to be known for making the right decisions under duress and being a good role model. To me, leadership is part of that but it is not the only aspect.

If the concept of leading is daunting to you and blocking your path, perhaps focus on being the best you can be in the moment. You may find people then gravitate towards you, asking for advice and direction. Without knowing it, you're quietly becoming a leader. It is about so much more than job titles.

Wherever you are on your leadership journey, be actively conscious that everyone is unique with myriad qualities. Learn about your team, find out what makes them tick, what demotivates them, what scares them, create the right environment, build trust and empower them. Then see what happens.

CHAPTER 8

NAVIGATING CHANGE

MANDY: Your path could be defined by the decision you make in the next few minutes. Will you go left or right? Will you stick or twist? Will you read on, turning the pages in rapt attention, or put the book down and go and do something else? We make decisions all the time, but some are more crucial to moving forward than others. Taking this job over that one will have more of a bearing on your future path than choosing between tea or coffee. The actual mechanics of making that decision are complex, ranging from weighing up the pros and cons, evaluating the perceived consequences and listening to your gut.

We've probably all written down a list of positives and negatives for a big decision at some point, trying to work out if the 'stats' show that one way is a clear no-no or the other way a no-brainer.

A lot of the airlines teach a decision-making acronym known as DODAR (Diagnosis, Options, Decide, Assign tasks, Review). British Airways adds a T to the start – do we have 'Time' to even go through this mental checklist? Often you don't, but having the DODAR framework is a handy mental back up. Some decisions are process-driven and you can practice for them. As a Tornado pilot we flew training sorties constantly to hone not just our skills but our decision-making mechanism.

By layering more and more complexity onto the training, we not only built-up resilience to the stress and workload through experience but we grooved our decision-making so that we had processes for every scenario.

Once, during the last phase of training in the UK before heading for an operational tour in the Gulf, my navigator and I made the mistake of dropping a very expensive live bomb on what we thought was the correct target, an orange life raft floating in the sea off the coast of Wales. Watching the film back later, we realised we had wasted our 1,000 lb bomb on a foaming wave. If we couldn't positively identify the target through our thermal imaging equipment, the correct decision would have been to abort the bombing run and come home. Later out in Kuwait we took off in a four-ship, armed with live ammunition for a bombing mission on a specified target deep into Iraq.

This time there were real people and politics at play so as we approached the vicinity of the target, my navigator and I were all business.

"Twenty seconds to target." That was my job as the driver.

"Continue. Not positively identified." That was the nav, looking through his thermal imaging camera, poised to 'mark' the target for the laser-guided Paveway bomb to hit.

"Ten seconds."

"Not positively identified."

"Five seconds."

"Not identified."

"Abort."

The decision was straightforward; there was no emotion

involved. We hadn't identified the target; therefore, we weren't going to drop the bomb. I'd learned my lesson from Wales.

Decision-making models like DODAR are all very well and clever but in our own lives in the real world they might be less useful. Firstly, that's because plenty of decisions we have to make come out of left field, so we're not practised at them. Secondly, we're emotional beings not always disposed to run through some management consultant-style checklist. And finally, it's the actual 'decide' part that ties us up in knots.

That's because we attempt to forecast all likely scenarios and from there plot our likely future path, potholes and all. We start conjuring up all the what ifs, the old fears of failure we discussed earlier. What if it doesn't work? What if I'm rubbish? (The answer to that, of course, is: What if it does? What if you are brilliant?) The bigger the decisions get – in terms of our perception of the magnitude of the consequences – the harder they are to make.

Some people are better at it than others. Some can make a quick analysis, come to a decision and move on, happy in their ability to deal with whatever cards they are then dealt. Others can't operate like that or would be horrified by this seemingly reckless approach and prefer a more cautious strategy, weighing up a decision from all aspects and strangling themselves with indecision. Sometimes the same person can take on both personas, depending on the nature of the decision.

Often, when people worry about a decision and delay making it, it is because they are scared of getting it 'wrong' or think (or know) they will look back wistfully and second guess their choice. Only hindsight will tell you whether it was the 'right' decision, but even that is spurious logic because you will never know how things would have panned out if you had taken a different option, nor could you have accurately predicted what would happen around the corner on the path you chose. Deciding to leave the RAF was tough and I agonised over what might be next. I could never have foreseen that I would go on to be a successful public speaker or be awarded the 'Champion of Women' at the Veterans in Business awards.

If I'd known, it might have made the decision much easier but only hindsight can tell you that.

I've always believed that being decisive is one of the most underrated leadership traits. People love a big strategy document or a vision board, but sometimes what you really need is someone who can make a call, especially under pressure, with half the facts and double the consequences. That's why I loved a session I once attended with Caspar Berry, a professional poker player turned business speaker. He didn't talk in corporate jargon or throw up fifty PowerPoint slides (okay, he did, but they were mainly great pictures).

He just talked about cards and risk. It was some of the best leadership advice I've ever heard. Caspar's take was simple: every hand of poker is a decision. Do you fold, call or raise? You rarely have all the information.

You can't know what cards the other players are holding. All you have is your own hand, your experience and a bit of gut instinct. Good decision-making, he said, is not about the outcome. It's about the process.

We judge so many of our decisions based on how it worked out, whether we got the result we wanted. If not, we berate ourselves for making a wrong call. That definition of a 'right' and 'wrong' decision is where we tie ourselves up in knots. Caspar pointed out that sometimes in poker you make the 'right' decision, based on all the information available to you at the time, and still lose.

That doesn't make it a 'bad' decision. The flip side is that you might make a 'terrible' decision, going against all perceived information and logic, and get lucky. Luck, however, isn't a strategy. The key is making the best call you can with what you've got, in that moment.

Caspar said the biggest mistake people make is playing not to lose instead of playing to win. Hearing this made me smile as it sums up how I often play tennis these days. It's so easy to go safe and hit the ball back into the middle of the court, waiting for a more optimal moment to try for a winner. Sometimes you just have to commit and the same goes for life.

Caspar described professional poker players folding what might be a strong hand, because they've calculated the odds and the risk isn't worth it. That takes guts, especially when you've already put in some chips. In psychology, that's called the sunk cost fallacy, continuing with a course of action purely because you've already invested time, money or effort. But that sunk cost has no bearing on what might happen in the future.

In poker and business, that's often the path to failure.

The message is that decision-making is a skill that can be honed and developed, like building a muscle. It is a process, not a moment in isolation. Sure, we can all point to examples where a single decision changed everything, but in reality, that singular moment was part of a bigger narrative. As Caspar says, you don't need to be right every time.

Make your decision and then react accordingly. If that means making another decision to get closer to the outcome you were after, try to make it a 'good' one and move on.

A perfect example of this was when I was approached by a major publishing house to re-publish my first book and write a second one – something I had dreamed of doing for years. On paper, this should have been an easy decision. My logical brain was saying, "This is it. The big break. A well-known publisher wants to take your book, promote it, and distribute it worldwide. Why would you even hesitate?"

I imagined the grand book launch, the PR team, the media coverage. But the reality of the situation was very different. I had a lot going on personally with two teenage boys struggling at school, aging and sick parents and an already hectic speaking schedule.

Even though my head was saying, "Take the deal, this is what you've always wanted," there was a nagging doubt deep in my soul. I researched the process around publishing and listed the pros and cons of going it alone vs handing over my intellectual property to the publishing house. But that just fed the virus and I went about my business feeling as if I was dragging a ball and chain of indecision behind me. I would lie awake for hours at night churning the various scenarios around in my head.

Even when I did get some sleep I would wake up, experience a few seconds of neutral thought bliss and then bang, in flooded the wave of angst again, like teenagers gatecrashing a party. I was permanently tense and tired and felt as if I was peering out at life through the narrow slit of a post-box as the worries closed in around me.

Eventually, I ran out of time to dither and had to decide. Shaking as I picked up the phone, I told the publishing house I would be politely declining their offer. They were taken aback but I've never once looked back on it with regret. In the end, I trusted myself.

Instead of doing what I thought I should do, I did what was right for me. This experience reinforced an important truth: decision-making isn't just about logic and choosing the best option; it's about choosing the best option for you, in that moment. Emotionally and physically. And sometimes, that means trusting yourself, even when others don't understand your choice.

That decision is just like points on a railway, directing you down another track. Whatever happens on the other side is a whole new adventure waiting to unfold.

CRAIG: Even though we flew some routes very regularly there is no such thing as a routine flight. One morning I reported for duty ready to captain our aircraft on a four-sector day in and out of Gatwick to a couple of destinations in Europe. Reading through the technical log of the Airbus A320 I had been assigned; I noticed the aircraft had a faulty fire loop detector on engine two. Sometimes if items of equipment don't work correctly you can carry them as an acceptable defect.

In terms of threat management, you've identified it and can then decide if the threat is manageable. The Airbus A320 has two engines and clearly you couldn't set off with just one working. But because each engine has two fire loop detectors, which light up in the cockpit if there is a fire, and because engines are very reliable and a fire would be an unusual event, it is acceptable to set off with one loop out per engine as a defect. The technical log gives the history of the aircraft, its flying hours, defects, repairs, planned repairs and in this case procedures to follow for the inoperative fire loop.

Other crews may have decided against taking out this aircraft, but we did all the checks we needed to and ran through various what-if scenarios and decided we were happy it was okay to fly.

We flew one sector out and were cruising back to Gatwick somewhere over France when the electronic centralised aircraft monitor (ECAM) lit up to tell me there was an additional fault, the second loop in engine 2 had failed. There was no indication of a fire, just that the fire loop sensors weren't working. Now we had a bit of a problem as both fire detection loops in that engine were now out of action. But what did this really mean? Everything else seemed fine and, in our opinion, there was no reason at this stage to divert the flight.

Clearly there would be a problem when we landed at Gatwick as they couldn't dispatch it with two fire loops out, but that didn't really worry us because we were going there anyway. The first officer and I decided for now we would carefully monitor the instruments rather than relying on the flight warning computer.

We flew on, senses heightened a little as we scanned the dials for any sign of an issue, but all seemed fine. About ten minutes later the red ECAM fire alert, a 'Master Warning' lit up to say we had a fire on engine two. Crikey. Now we really did have a problem.

Although flights can be very mundane, when things happen, they happen quite quickly and you have to be ready to make a decision. A reasonable course of action would be to consider shutting down the engine due to the ECAM warning. You can fly on a single engine but you can't maintain height at 35,000 feet as you have insufficient power so you gradually drift down, meaning we'd be unable to reach Gatwick and would have to divert to an airport en route. It's not unusual to fly on a single engine and it's something we practise regularly.

But we faced a dilemma. What's the right call here, Craig old boy? Do we follow the ECAM and shut down the engine or keep it running?.

The number one priority is always to ensure the safety of the aircraft and its passengers without further consequences. But diverting an aircraft also puts in place a chain of events that would have ramifications for the airline, the passengers and us down the line. The aircraft would be in the wrong location, the options for repairs and support at the new airfield might be limited and the passengers would need assistance in completing their journey. So, what to do when we know the fire detection system is faulty and unreliable? Shutdown the engine or challenge the process? It is a big decision.

You have to understand the consequences of your actions. If you keep it running and there is a fire – which is one of the most severe things that can happen on an aircraft – you potentially have about twelve minutes before the fire is out of control and the aircraft won't survive. So, we're not talking about unlimited time to make the decision.

In the old days before clever flight computers, pilots had to use airmanship and monitor the instruments to assess the health of an engine, looking at a change in the temperature, fuel flow, a loss of power, loss of thrust or any vibrations. If any of these parameters had changed, I'd have called for an immediate divert to land at Bordeaux. But our instruments weren't suggesting anything was amiss, so why would you shut it down when you've got no confirmation? You could be shutting down an engine which is perfectly serviceable, knowing you can't rely on the fire warning system. Is that a great idea?

I've since used this dilemma as a learning point for students. What would you do? When I put the question to them in the classroom, the room is generally split half and half. Actually, it's sort of a trick question because there is arguably no right or wrong answer. I'd say you're wrong if you say, "Listen to the ECAM and shut down the engine".

I'd also say you're wrong if you decide to ignore it and keep the engine running. You need to challenge your thought process, and make sure to avoid confirmation bias. If it is a fire, then I have been trained and know how to deal with it. But we are not that well trained in dilemma.

We feel uncomfortable. A big problem in a small cockpit is how do you keep together as a team if one pilot wants to carry out one action and the other prefers a different option? It could quickly turn into a real issue in terms of negative dynamics, cooperation, communication, efficiency and ultimately safety as we've seen. This is where CRM training is crucial. As a captain I'd always ask the first officer what they think.

I'd ask in a particular way, too. I wouldn't give a leading question or state my preference first because they might be overwhelmed and think well, Craig is much more experienced, he's the captain so I'll just agree. That's not the best outcome. It's better to ask open questions so they are free to answer in their own way.

When I pose this question in the classroom it's always fascinating to see people's reactions. They often get pretty animated and have some heated discussions, which is great. In the cockpit you don't have time for that. You need to reach a decision much more efficiently.

I called the senior cabin crew member and asked her to stroll down the back and have a surreptitious glance out of the windows either side to see what she could see of the engines. I deliberately didn't send the first officer as that could have caused undue alarm, nor did I mention the word fire as I wanted a completely objective opinion. Also asking a non-technical staff member to make a fairly large call on an engine is not a smart move. A few minutes later she came back into the cockpit saying everything looked fine.

So now it was decision time. Heed the fire warning and shut down the engine despite no evidence of a fire, or carry on with the threat hanging over us? Fortunately, the first officer and I seemed to be on the same page, and our decision was to carry on with the engine running.

I tasked him with flying the aircraft while I eyeballed the instruments, ready to review the decision and change our plan if we needed to. What might have been a good decision a few minutes ago might not be now if the instruments showed something. We flew on, quiet, alert and hyper-focused on the instruments, braced to act should the situation change. Please lights, stay as you are.

Be good to us. After about ten minutes the red fire warning sign went out, which gave us a bit more confidence that we had an unreliable system. We continued to Gatwick; happy we would have the passengers in the right place and the aircraft back at base for technical support. You might disagree with our decision and that's fine, but that's the decision we made at the time based on the information available to us.

You need to work through the problem and justify the consequences. I'd probably do the same thing today. The other important factor for me to justify our decision was that the A320 always gets you to 'Confirm the Failure' before carrying out any ECAM actions. Since we were unable to do this, it supported our decision to keep the engine running.

So you can see, even in aviation, decision-making is not an exact science. You can't always input the variables and have some tool spit out the answer. Sure, you can DODAR the heck out of it or compile columns of pros and cons, but ultimately decision-making is an art and relies on human intuition and human logic, flawed or otherwise. How many times have you ordered food in a restaurant and then looked around the table and realised you've got food envy, that you've made the 'wrong' call? As we have seen, it's not wrong, it's just a decision.

Put it behind you or change your attitude to your meal and move on. The bigger the decisions get – in terms of our perception of the magnitude of the consequences – the harder they are to make. When I eventually left EasyJet, I couldn't have known that that would be the last time I captained an Airbus A320 in the air as opposed to a simulator but that is how the path worked out. I'm at peace with that, but it may have got in the way of my decision-making process at the time.

If you change paths often, like in the military, you're likely to be better able to accept that nothing is forever. Therefore, when it comes to making decisions about your future direction, you recognise that there is no such thing as a bad decision, just a different path. Escalators delivering you somewhere new, with fresh challenges ahead. Make your best decision at the time, then make it a good one by responding accordingly.

If you don't like the outcome, fix it. If you do, crack on.

CHAPTER 9

AEROBATICS

MANDY: Clutching the stick lightly in my right hand I ease it forward to lower the nose and gain speed before pulling it hard back towards me. At the same time, I suck in a quick breath and tense my stomach, my butt and my leg muscles to accept the G-force. Oof, here it comes... I... can't... move... I'm being thrust into the seat by a great weight, like being at the bottom of a bundle at school. My head is being squeezed, and my cheeks are pinned to my ears.

The nose of the aircraft rapidly rises through the horizon and continues up through shades of blue until it is pointing into space, laying me on my back with my feet above my head. I hold the stick in my sternum, making sure I keep the wings level. I can feel the blood flooding my head and making my eyes bulge as I surge towards the stratosphere.

I keep pulling, looking over my head, as the nose tips over the top of the loop pointing our belly to the stars. Keep coming, over, over, there's the horizon again... I'm now facing directly down at the ground through the canopy, free falling as my shoulders thrust forward on the seat straps. Oosh, there goes my stomach. I quite like the sensation, but the elevator drop is only fleeting as we shallow out of our dive to complete the loop.

At the bottom the airframe shakes violently, but I smile. Nice one. That means we've hit our own turbulent air and have described a perfect circle. I level out, allowing my eyes to refocus and then push the stick forward again.

The nose dips below the horizon and we pick up speed before I pull back and nudge the control column to my right thigh to put the wings at 45 degrees to the horizon. I keep pulling and my hand moves back up my thigh until I tip onto my side and then go inverted. Upside down, the distant clouds now look like white puddles beneath a green sky. Keeping the stick to the right, my eyes are fixed on the rotating horizon as the aircraft corkscrews around it.

As we come out of it, I trace the column across to my left thigh to keep manoeuvre going and then back to the middle to complete a barrel roll.

Now time for my favourite, a variation of a stall turn called a Noddy. Nose down, accelerate... 140 knots, 150, 160... and up. I pull back hard, sending us towards the moon. G time.

Oof. Inhale, tense everything and feel the force. I inch the stick forward to keep the aircraft vertical and stop us falling over backwards. When I sense the speed is dropping, I press my left foot down to apply full left rudder.

This nods the nose of the aircraft violently to the left, cutting cleanly so the nose of the aircraft hits the horizon, I release my left foot and stamp on the right rudder pedal with my other foot, nodding it to the right. We're falling tail first now. Another full left kick brings the nose around and we're facing directly back down towards the ground. A few seconds of freefall and big G-force squidges my cheeks and puts my head in a vice before I ease back on the stick to level us out before the next manoeuvre.

In practice I'm not thinking about each step in the

aerobatics display. I am at one with the aircraft, flying instinctively, in tune with its quirks, capabilities and limits, woman and machine melded into one being. I am like a skilled musician whose soul speaks through their instrument as I tumble and turn around the sky. Not thinking, just doing.

An aerial dancer encased in metal. Sports people talk about being in the zone. This is the pilot's zone. The practice, the training, the procedures, the checklists, the rational thoughts, the threat and error management and human factors are moulded into a high-functioning individual.

Often, though, we humans are not in the zone and need help to become the full package. That goes as much for leaders as it does for other team members. To get to a place of high performance of course requires the skills, but it also requires honesty, trust and a willingness to put your ego on the line for the greater good of the team. That's when a good debrief comes in.

One of my last ever flights in the RAF was with the Red Arrows. For an aviation nut it was a dream day out, even for someone who had flown a much faster, more powerful aircraft in the Tornado. I'd scored a ride in the back seat of one of the famous red Hawks and experienced a full display, complete with red, white and blue smoke and somewhere down on the ground, the crowd oohing and aahing at our antics. Rocking and rolling with the Reds was like being right there, on the pitch, standing next to your favourite players as they went about their business.

My face hurt from grinning.

But what really stood out was the debrief afterwards. It's an open environment and there were a host of other civilians in the room, such as prize winners and sponsors, but the debrief was completely authentic, not at all for show.

It started with the leader, Red 1, admitting and apologising for a mistake. This immediately role modelled that it is fine to be vulnerable and that this is a safe environment for open and honest feedback.

Then they watched a playback of the performance, stopping regularly if one of the team spotted an error or wanted to discuss an aspect of the flight and any learnings to take forward.

"Why did you turn in there, mate?" or "You were a bit late on that one."

Each pilot had their own performance critiqued. It was clear they all appreciated and respected their team-mates' honesty. No one judged or apportioned blame. It was never a finger-pointing exercise.

It was all about the behaviour not the personality. If there was an issue it was all about what had happened, why it happened and how they were going to fix it for next time.

Many of us, if we are being honest, will admit to shying away from accountability at times. We've all become defensive at one time or another when our performance has been called into question. No one likes to feel as though they're being criticised by their colleagues or leaders, especially in a public setting.

But none of the Red Arrows pilots were getting defensive and fighting back, unwilling to be seen as less than stellar. All took their medicine in a mature fashion, objectively analysing their own performance, with the same brutal honesty as their peers, accepting the comments and noting the issues for next time.

"That wasn't brilliant, was it? Sorry about that" or "Yep, fair one, I need to make sure I hit that turning point perfectly. Got it. Cheers."

It wasn't all one way, either. There was praise when it was due. It can't all be nit-picking.

"Red 3, love your spacing, excellent job."

Looking around the room, I realised everyone in there was gripped. No one was snatching cheeky looks at phones or watches or windows. The honesty of the debrief had made it compelling and very human. No longer were these guys superheroes wrapped in red jets, they were just people doing a high-performing job and trying to get a bit better.

The act of debriefing helps us to cultivate that growth mindset which helps you maximise your effectiveness and achieve your full potential by viewing failure as a chance to improve. It's that 'just culture' again. Even if your leadership and performance objectives have been met and the project went well, a good debrief will empower your team to become even more efficient and effective. Even if it is just about a meeting you've had, have a quick conflab with your colleagues afterwards about what went well, what could we do less of, what could we do more of? A debrief should always be led by a good facilitator but it doesn't have to be the most senior person in the room.

In the military we have a phrase 'Leave your stripes at the door'. I have actually seen leaders physically remove their stripes from their epaulets to make the point that there is no hierarchy within the debrief. It's really important to set the right tone at the start of the debrief, perhaps explaining that this is a safe environment in which everyone will be heard. It's also a good idea to have a clear idea beforehand what you want to cover and outline this at the start.

A key framework of the debrief funnel is to start with the facts. What was supposed to happen and what actually happened? Next, we need to understand the cause of what happened, good or bad. This is the 'why'. Smart, open questions can dig further down to reach the answers.

Hopefully, you will then arrive as a team at the 'how'. The cure. Notice again how there is no 'who'. It is not about who is right, but about what is right.

When I ask organisations why they don't debrief, I always hear it's because they don't have time. Adding one more thing to the regular routine might be the straw that breaks the camel's back, they moan. But if your ultimate objective is to remain relevant, achieve big goals and continuously learn and excel then the debrief is a powerful tool that can save you time and effort in the long run. You will cut down on errors, inefficiencies and angst and grow stronger, smarter and faster than your competition.

More commonly I hear that companies do debrief, but only when things go wrong. It's the 'post-mortem' philosophy, trying to find the root cause. But why not debrief when things go well too. Sharing best practice is a powerful tool.

Another useful trick is to run a pre-mortem. Get everyone in the team to imagine that you are three years down the line, looking back on the project and analysing why it didn't work well. Write down all the difficulties, all the limitations and then it will give you a framework to look at the potential threats that are waiting around the next corner.

CRAIG: When I was making my transition from military pilot to the commercial sector I had to take a simulator test as part of my interview process with GB Airways. The task was to take off in a 737, fly around a circuit and land back at the same airport.

It was an aircraft I had never flown or even sat in the cockpit, although I was given some simple parameters beforehand, like pitch and power for straight and level and a basic checklist including when to select flaps and the gear down. I did, at best, a reasonable job.

It could have been a bit better, but it could have been a lot worse.

"Well done, Craig, you've passed, but it's a real shame you let your speed drop off on the final approach," said the examiner.

At the time I was just delighted to have passed but looking back now as an experienced trainer I am disappointed he didn't get to the root cause of why I let the speed drop off. If the approach speed was supposed to be 140 knots and I landed at 135 knots, there could have been lots of reasons – I could have been fixated on landing, my scan might have broken down or I got distracted or something else. As a military pilot you fly an approach speed but then slow down so that your speed over the threshold, that is the final seconds of the approach to the runway at a height of about fifty feet, is five knots slower. Therefore, I had made a conscious action to reduce speed, but in the commercial world I discovered it is not done this way.

By not asking me about it, the trainer never understood why this happened and could reasonably suspect it was a handling issue. A facilitated debrief would have been an ideal platform to dig into this a bit more. He could have asked me questions specific to the landing, such as what speed did you land at? If I replied with 135 knots then he would have realised I was aware of my speed, so probably not a scan issue then. Next, he could ask why did you land at 135 knots when the approach speed was 140 knots? Now we are drilling down to the real reason behind the error.

For me, it was a knowledge issue, not a skill issue.

It was an example of a leader, in this case the instructor, falling back on preconceived ideas and assuming there is a problem that doesn't exist; in my case it wasn't an ability to hold my speed through aircraft handling, but a lack of knowledge of the operating procedure. I wonder how many debriefs you've been in when the real cause of something happening was left unresolved. A good debrief should be honest, open and conducted in an environment where everyone feels comfortable and can use their voice, not embarrassed or belittled for making mistakes. It must be structured, though, this is not a coffee morning or time to chew the fat.

Timing is important. If it has been a tough assignment, give people space. Give them a chance to organise their thoughts so they are more structured in their heads and better able to reflect on their performance. Often people assume a debrief happens at the end of an action, but when we're training in the simulator, we will often conduct a 'hot debrief'.

Having said it is good to let people gather their thoughts, there is no point waiting two or three hours to go over a minor point that may become superseded by something more pressing but still needs to be discussed. Why waste that training opportunity? We might debrief one or two points there and then and move on. So, why did you turn on that heading? Why did you bring up the flaps?

Let's imagine this scenario for a moment. Craig and Mandy have been flying together. Craig has his examiners hat on. Let's consider this as his examiner's assessment after the test flight:

"Well, that wasn't great, was it? I suppose you've done the bare minimum to pass. I've seen lots of others do better. Your speed control in the final approach was shockingly inaccurate and you stalled the plane. I suppose the stall recovery was okay, and you landed without crashing so well done. To be honest though, you need to do better, or you are going to struggle here."

How would you feel about that debrief?

Mandy: I would be happy I passed, but all I would have heard was negativity. There wasn't a single question. It just felt like I was being talked at. There was no opportunity for reflection.

No learning points.

Craig: It was all about the instructor instilling their own superiority. No one got anything out of it. How about this instead:

"Mandy, why don't you get a coffee and when you are ready, we'll sit down and have a debrief".

"Well done, Mandy, another successful detail, some nice positive aspects of flight but what I'm really interested in initially is, which bits of the flight did you think went well?"

Mandy: "I thought the upper air work was good, my aerobatics were spot on, my speed control was okay, joining the circuit was good."

Craig: "Yes, that was really nice, you planned that well, got the aircraft in the right place at the right time so well done for that. What about that penultimate circuit?"

Mandy: "That wasn't so good."

Craig: "Why not?"

Mandy: "It was looking good, I was in the right position at the end of the downwind leg and as I turned in, I remember thinking the wind had picked up, so I started to overbank the aircraft a bit. So then I had the wind blowing into me, a tightening wind. I don't think I added enough power."

Craig: "Why did that happen? What was the cause?"

Mandy: "One was wind, a big one was other aircraft. I could hear ATC talking, I could hear another aircraft joining the circuit. I wasn't entirely sure where it was, and I could feel myself getting distracted at the critical time when I should have been 100 per cent focused on flying the aircraft."

Craig: "Some good points there. Let's just go back to the facts. Turning on to finals, what happened when your air speed became low?"

Mandy: "The stall warning went off which required an immediate action, so I did the standard stall recovery, control column centrally forward (to reduce the angle of attack), rolled the wings level, applied full power and climbed away from the ground to a minimum safe altitude."

Craig: "You did really well in that. So how can we fix it, what is the cure to help prevent you from getting distracted in the circuit next time?"

Mandy: "I need to be more vigilant about the threats at this critical stage of flight to ensure that I don't end up in this position again. I have a way forward and some excellent learning points to build on. Thank you."

Craig: "So Mandy how are feeling now after the second debrief?"

Mandy. "It was constructive, I didn't feel threatened, there was real value in self discovering some areas which I need to focus on, but there were also some really positive points about my overall performance. Away from the formal debrief, I will spend some time reflecting on the 2 or 3 points and will hopefully be able to use them on my next flight."

These are two very different styles of debrief, one instructional, the other more constructive, where the recipient has time to understand, accept and is therefore better equipped to move forward. You decide which style works best.

CRAIG: The grind was getting me down. Teaching on the job as a line training captain was rewarding but after several years the relentless nature of the work was draining everything I had, professionally and personally. Flying four flights a day is gruelling enough but when you have a training component on top of your responsibilities as a captain it becomes almost unsustainable. I've always thought it is a bit daft to have the most inexperienced trainers in this line training captain role.

After all, the greatest risk is in the actual aircraft where real things can go wrong and you have actual people on board, and yet the higher up the training ladder you go, the more time you spend exclusively in the simulator. It is one of those legacy situations that has not been challenged, but with the more progressive thinking behind human factors in aviation, it really should be.

One way to escape the grind and keep my path moving was to tackle the dreaded type-rating instructor (TRI) course which lets you instruct on the specific aircraft types. The course has a fearsome reputation for failing large numbers of candidates and it had been looming like a billowing black cloud on my path. After passing an initial interview to even be accepted on the course I began prepping months ahead. The course was over two weeks, based at EasyJet's facility in Burgess Hill with EasyJet trainers.

The course has this somewhat elevated reputation of only the best of the best get through, a bit like my old SMAC Harrier conversion days, which is ridiculous. If you have the desire and the ability to teach, and if you have been a line training captain, you should have all the core competencies. It's a more technical course than line training, taking in complicated scenarios involving hydraulics, electrics, engines or other functions, rather than the more practical aspects of dealing with passengers or weather avoids which you would encounter on the line. When you become a trainer, the trainee may ask you about all these technical aspects and you need to have a good understanding of how it works.

You also need to be able to explain it confidently, standing up in front of a white board or smart board looking like Captain all-the-answers. I was acutely conscious of my academic background and turned up each morning apprehensive and on edge, feeling like the smallest mistake would be punished. It began with some technical tests, introductions to teaching for those who hadn't been instructors and classroom work where we were supposed to showcase our ability to explain and communicate in front of others. It then moved into the simulator with a trainer playing the role of trainee and you as the training instructor overseeing various scenarios and guiding them through their deliberate mistakes and issues.

One area that drained a lot of capacity even before starting training was operating the sim. It's second nature to me now, but it can be perplexing at first and diminishes the quality of training because you're focused on making the kit work. One time I just couldn't get the blooming thing to operate and had to call a halt to the session. The technician came in and pointed out I had pressed the big red illuminated button saying, 'Flight freeze'.

Every night I sat hunched over the desk in my hotel room prepping hard for the next day. I was comfortable with the instructing and communicating but trying to cram some of the more technical aspects into my head was fueling mild panic and I could feel my shoulders tightening by the minute. This manifested into less than stellar performances in front of the white board, floundering when grilled further on certain points.

I knew I was sinking but that just made it worse. I was existing in a nether world, somewhere between the real me and a confused, embattled, uncertain version. Several days before the final assessment my trainer took me to one side and suggested he didn't think I was ready to take the test. I sort of agreed with him and left the course, somewhat relieved to escape the intense environment, but bitterly disappointed.

It's a tough course, and clearly you need to reach the required standard, but I felt the atmosphere was overly oppressive. Like SMAC 309 all over again, I had not responded well to the environment. What I say to trainees now is that it's not the mistakes I'm interested in so much as whether you understand them enough to be able to fix them. As a trainer it is your responsibility to ensure the environment is right to train.

You need to think about what the trainee wants and whether you are appealing to their preferred learning style. It's important to understand that everyone learns in a different way.

Another interesting thing from a training and personnel development point of view is that no one from the airline got in touch to see how I was or try to understand what the problem was with one of their line training captains. Let's face it; if you manage to get onto the course in the first place you're already at a certain standard and should effectively be ready to go. The failure rate should be really small, otherwise you are recruiting the wrong people for the course.

This setback essentially defined the rest of my time at EasyJet. I grudgingly went back to the day job and the energy-sapping slog of it all. I knew I would never take the course again there and so it felt like I was stagnating with no way forward. I managed to reduce my flying rota, but I knew I wouldn't be happy continuing just as a line trainer with this TRI failure hanging over me.

I needed to find another route around the problem.

I got chatting to a pilot friend named Andy Mitchell, a super talented aviator with a brain the size of a planet. Andy had wanted to be a military pilot, but he had eyesight issues and went the airline route, ending up at GB Airways before it was bought by EasyJet. He's about twenty years younger than me but we became good friends and kept in touch with each other's careers. We both had this TRI itch that needed scratching, so we hatched a plan to team up and do the course together, self-funded at CTC pilot training academy in Southampton.

It was still hard work but by effectively joining forces we tackled it together, helping each other out and providing moral support. The independent tutors had a totally different mindset, they appeared to be on your side, willing to try to get the best out of you, rather than destroy you, without compromising safety. It was still intense and tough, but Andy and I passed. Even so, I knew my EasyJet days were coming to an end.

I just didn't have the stomach for it anymore. The punishing schedule, the demands of line training and just sheer fatigue were eroding my personal buffer in terms of standards. I brought it up with the company, but its response was to give me more training in the simulator. I didn't need more training; I needed less flying and a more sympathetic roster.

I was struggling to keep up the momentum to be an enthusiastic, capable and effective trainer all day, every day.

My training approach was to demonstrate a particular manoeuvre or sector and then get the trainee to repeat it. On a four-sector day with all things being equal in terms of weather, route and other variables, I generally flew the first sector and then let the trainee fly the next two as I observed, with me flying the final sector home to give the trainee a rest, given they were also generally working to capacity. The trouble was, by now I was knackered too.

The nail in the coffin came one day when we were flying back to Gatwick. The weather was benign, and the trainee was doing really well so I let him fly the final sector home. I was supposed to be monitoring him as he flew the approach, but when air traffic control came on the radio to say, "Clear to land", I should have replied, "Roger, clear land, Easy A25T." Instead, I was miles away, just gazing out of the window, thinking about tennis or drumming or something. The controller repeated his line, and again I failed to acknowledge.

When he said it a third time, the trainee interrupted my reverie.

"I think they're just after confirmation that we're clear to land."

Then the voice came on again, insistent, urging. "I say again, you are cleared to land. Acknowledge, acknowledge."

This jolted me out of whatever vacant space I had been exploring in my head. Wow, it's come to this. Not only can you not respond to a single air traffic control command, but you're also certainly not monitoring the trainee to a level that a new pilot deserves. Fortunately, he went on to land as smoothly as a seasoned aviator.

Not long after this incident I came to the final decision and handed in my resignation. I still had a thirst for training, so I joined CTC as a consultant. The next logical step was to become a type-rating examiner (TRE) which is the level that assesses pilots' licences, from their initial Licence Skills Test (LST) to their ongoing Licence Proficiency Check (LPC) which is every twelve months.

The TRE course is actually more straightforward than the TRI course and covers a lot of rules and regulations about training such as the fact that most proficiency checks are two-attempt tests, meaning if you struggle on one small aspect you can get some further training during the test and have another go, but if you fail the second time around then that is it. I passed without any issues and from TRE I took the course to become qualified as a training standards captain to ensure the trainers are all up to scratch and teaching to the same high levels. I would sit in the sim and assess them as they trained, with focused debriefs and learning points afterwards to enhance their effectiveness. With each step up the training rung I was focusing more on my real areas of interest.

I'm fascinated by how instructors approach the whole training discipline. Are you going to go down the bad cop route and teach with fear? If so, what results are you expecting to get from that? If I was the student, it would never end well. Or are you striving to become a trainer who sets an environment to get the best out of the trainee and promotes growth and development? In my view a trainee should never feel threatened in the simulator or any training environment. It should not be a case of thinking I could lose my licence by the end of this afternoon, although occasionally it happens, and for good reason.

I've failed a few people in my time, not many, and it is never a great moment, but you have to do the right thing. If you deliver the message in the right way and earn their buy-in that they haven't yet reached the right standard, then you can hopefully turn it into some sort of positive and reassure them that this is part of the learning process and that it is not unusual to require additional support.

As a type-rating examiner I had one guy who struggled from the start. He had already failed his first test completely and I was tasked to run his second test. He was enthusiastic and trying really hard, but it became pretty obvious during the skills test he was not going to make it. It is a two-attempt test but during the second attempt he asked to do one manoeuvre again so he knew in his own mind that this particular task had room for improvement.

In the end I just stopped the sim and said we need to review a few of these things before we move forward. I was 100% certain in my decision to fail him. Sometimes it is a marginal call but with this guy I knew. He knew deep down too.

I didn't do it lightly; I was well aware of the devastating impact it would have on him and his career. He would have invested heavily in time and money getting to this stage, but it is not my role to get involved in his future path, that's up to him and the training organisation, although they would ask for my opinion. In reality, he should not have even got that far. I'm there to assess whether he is up to scratch to move forward, with safety always as the number one priority.

If I passed him, I would be shunting the problem down the line.

I had another candidate who came from a military background. He was a Royal Navy pilot like me, and he was good. At one point I simulated an engine failure, so he had to fly a glide approach with no engine. If you are not in exactly the right configuration for landing, you should make the decision to go around and try again.

He was gliding in at very low level with quite a lot of angle of bank, meaning the aircraft was tilting over. At about fifty feet above the ground, he had thirty degrees of bank. He was wrestling with the controls and trying his hardest to get the aircraft on the runway, and in a manner of speaking he did manage to stick it on the tarmac. I failed him for it and he began arguing, adamant he was right and that he had pulled off the landing, so what was the problem?.

The whole point is that it is a safety check requiring you to make the right decisions, not a rodeo. He wasn't some bush pilot trying to make an emergency landing or a Huey chopper pilot trying to get his bird down in a jungle clearing in a firefight. It was him and me in a metal box anchored via hydraulic legs to the ground. The safe decision here would have been to throw away the approach and try again.

He just couldn't accept it. I've met him a few times since and he still refers back to it. But I maintain that if at some later stage he did the same for real and speared his wing into the ground he could have killed himself and others. I would have to live with that.

Failing someone is hard because you are painfully aware of the time and financial commitment these people have put into aviation as their career. These days it costs about £120,000 to become a commercial airline pilot from scratch, and by the time you've added everything else on top it is probably realistically more like £150,000. That is a significant amount of money in anyone's trousers and one of the reasons, therefore, that you shouldn't have to undergo irrelevant training just to tick an outdated box. What makes a competent pilot anyway? Is it that you can fly an approach at plus or minus fifty feet and within five to ten knots of the prescribed speed? Those things are important, of course, and are still a key requirement, but the real answer is that you need a lot of other skills.

You need to be able to make quality decisions, manage an intense and varied workload, be able retain a wide situational awareness and communicate clearly with people. But for decades training has been focused on specific skills which have now become outdated as aircraft have become more reliable. The threats that existed before, particularly mechanical, have become increasingly obsolete with modern technology, which in turn has brought with it a new set of threats.

On modern jet aircraft, engine failure is less of a problem than it was. It can still occur, of course, with tragic consequences, but I don't know anyone in forty years of flying who has suffered an actual engine failure and had to manually fly a single-engine go-around, where you have to abort a landing and reconfigure your approach on one engine. And yet performing the correct actions for such an eventuality is a huge prerequisite for traditional pilot testing where it is pass or fail. If I flew a simulated engine failure after take-off and momentarily dropped my speed by a few knots, I could fail the test.

Are you really going to take away my licence for that? This is not about lessening standards, of course, but imagine how many different technical scenarios could come up. There are probably about 2500–3000 permutations of failure in an Airbus A320. Are you going to know the correct procedure for every single one? If you tried to test for each one on the type rating course, you would be there for years. Instead, it should be all about the whole environment, taking a holistic view of the individual to assess whether or not they are competent and able to react appropriately, alongside being able to fly the aircraft.

With this in mind, the industry moved towards competency training, developing a framework of nine competencies that pilots must demonstrate:.

1. Flight path management, automatic.
2. Flight path management, manual.
3. Communication.
4. Workload management.
5. Situational awareness.
6. Knowledge application.
7. Problem solving.
8. Application of procedures.
9. Leadership and teamwork.

Drilling into these, it is about your associated behaviours for each one. For example, as a trainer I can't just say to a pilot they need to be a better communicator. They need to display observable behaviours. If a pilot was to ask his colleague: "Are you ready to brief? okay, we are about to crash..." That's communicating, but it's not much help.

It is about how you communicate, what you say, to whom and when and how you process your side of the communication. Do you listen actively, patiently and demonstrate understanding? Appropriate use of body language, tone and other forms of non-verbal communication are also important, which goes back to the human factors element. Equally, the flight path management manual stipulates a pilot is competent at controlling an aircraft manually and accurately, so you can't just be a good communicator and fabulous at making decisions if you then steer it straight into the sea. It is all part of a bigger picture.

It is less about a series of check tests which you can pass or fail and more about the trainer taking a broader view and asking themselves the question: is this person competent as a pilot?

To my way of thinking this is a substantial leap forward, but the real rocket fuel is evidence-based training (EBT). This is competency training on steroids. Rather than relying on legacy methods, it uses real threats which are presented to pilots based on the type of aircraft they are flying. The airlines and the industry as a whole have been gathering data on threats and failures for decades and have segmented the data for different generations of aircraft.

The Airbus A320 is what is known as Generation Four so the threats are very different to a Generation One aircraft such as a turboprop for which the threats would be based on mechanical failure.

Andy Mitchell became very interested in evidence-based training and co-founded a company called Empower EBT. He asked me to help out and apart from the initial core instructors, I became the first International Air Transport Association (IATA) EBT-qualified instructor, mainly because I was on the first ever course and was sitting right at the front, so I was the first to be handed a certificate. Forward-thinking airlines have taken this concept of EBT on board, airlines such as Turkish Airlines, Air Baltic, British Airways, EasyJet, Air France and Iberia. Some have adopted it, others are reluctant for change or are mindful of the cost and complications with aviation regulators.

It continues to gather pace, however, and in my view is where the whole aviation industry should get to.

The broad concept is highly applicable outside aviation too. In essence it is an antidote to that most mind-numbing of phrases, "This is how we've always done it here". Well, guess what? There might be a better way of doing it. In your world – work or personal life – are there still legacy behaviours or long-held procedures? It might be time to reassess and see where you can improve. Challenging the system in a constructive way is another stepping stone on your path, requiring confidence, an inquiring mind, a desire to improve both personally and as a group and a willingness to speak up, in other words showing leadership.

Put them all together and you'll go from flying straight and level at low altitude to performing barrel rolls and Cuban eights high above the clouds.

CHAPTER 10

FINAL APPROACH

MANDY: Because you are a path-changer and a dynamic, switched-on individual, you will have spotted from the title of this chapter that the narrative arc of our flight is coming to an end. But really our philosophy is that there is no landing, no final destination. For us, it is about moving on, whether that is incrementally, like booking another course of drumming lessons, or via a huge reroute like leaving the military. It is about hopping on and off those moving, shifting escalators; some steep, some less so; some fast, some slower; some going in your chosen direction, others not so much but it could be interesting to see where they go.

At various points there are decisions to be made, hurdles to overcome, threats to be managed. There will be good times and bad. The key though, is to remember it is your story and your journey. You have the power to craft it, and because of that you can't get it wrong.

Sure, there might be things you would prefer to change but how you react to those is up to you. We all need help, guidance and advice along the way and luck always helps, but you are in control of you. There is no right way or wrong way, only your way. That's not to say you should ignore everyone else, but that you should absorb everything you see, hear and feel about the world around you and then react and make decisions suited to your circumstances.

Recently, I went on a mini break to Italy with some female friends. One day we went to Lake Garda and sauntered down to the water to rent one of the little motorboats anyone can take out without a licence. As we were filling in some paperwork, the female employee at the boat rental company asked where the man was.

"I'm sorry," I replied. "What do you mean?"

"Where is the man, who is with you?"

"Er, there is no man, it's just us."

"So, who is going to drive it?"

Flummoxed, I looked around at my companions. Let's see: it could be the consultant doctor and medical director; or maybe the chief people officer; or how about the CEO of a marketing consultancy? Or there's me I suppose, a former Tornado pilot in the RAF. Any of those do? The employee looked a bit mystified that there was no man but rented us the boat and we had a lovely time, all taking it in turns to drive after our comprehensive tutorial in the dock. We all took it as an amusing if predictable example of casual sexism and had a laugh about it over drinks that night.

After the trip I recounted the tale on LinkedIn, and it sparked an enormous response. Most people took it in the spirit I posted it and gave a figurative sigh and roll of the eyes before sharing other amusing (if you choose to react that way) stories of casual or even blatant sexism. A few took it literally and pointed out none of our accomplishments or titles made us automatically competent to drive a boat (these vessels required no qualifications). But a couple of comments made me stop and think again.

One person wrote that he had read my post to his Italian

wife, thinking she would find Italy's old-fashioned attitude to that sort of thing mildly funny. Instead, her reply surprised him and he asked her to repeat it so he could capture the response.

"People need to understand and respect national cultures without being judgemental," his wife said. "In Italy, a woman expects the man to look after her and to do all the heavy lifting. It's not a question of the boat company thinking the women couldn't possibly control the boat, it's the boat company wondering why these ladies didn't have men to look after them and ensure they didn't have to lift a finger. Italy is perfectly progressive in that women have the opportunities men have, but when doing something like this, the ladies would be expected to have the men spoiling them and treating them like royalty."

Clearly this is just one person's view and there may be other equally qualified Italian women with very different opinions. But it tilted my axis and got me really thinking. My take on the story was that it was just another classic, slightly annoying, very predictable but a bit funny if you choose not to get offended, case of casual sexism. But this lady's reaction was coming from a completely different place I hadn't considered.

It was more than just having a different opinion on something, such as, "Craig, this TV programme you are watching is rubbish." This was a whole paradigm shift in thinking, like peering into a different plane in the matrix. It showed how my view of the world is just one way of seeing things among myriad others, like one star in one galaxy of billions. If I'm open enough, the view I see through my prism of the world can be influenced by the light of others. And vice versa.

In Nepal, our merry band had settled into some kind of equilibrium as we plodded our way up through the Khumbu region below Everest. We trudged up the dusty trails all day and stayed in simple but cosy tea houses at night. We passed through the Sherpa villages of Tengboche, Dingboche and Lobuche to the outpost of Gorak Shep, the last settlement before base camp. It is a collection of low-rise stone buildings with mostly blue or green corrugated roofs on a sandy, frozen lakebed next to the Khumbu glacier which tumbles down from Everest.

From Gorak Shep, it is a further three-hour hike up a rock-strewn path through thinning air to base camp. Another night in Gorak Shep and then we woke at 0400 to climb the nearby hill of Kala Patthar, a stunning spot which gives spectacular sunrise views over the summit of Everest, which you can't see from base camp, and other Himalayan giants including Lhotse, Nuptse and Pumori.

From there it was all downhill, barring the numerous leg-burning ups, over a couple of days back to Namche Bazaar, the main hub of the Khumbu region, a town of blue, green and ochre-roofed buildings draped around the steep slopes of a horseshoe valley. Back in the relative metropolis, we headed out as a group to an Irish-themed bar to toast the trip. Most of us had a couple of drinks and headed back to our tea house at about seven o'clock for dinner before hitting the sack.

In the morning, the atmosphere at breakfast seemed weird. The few Wigan boys that were around seemed very quiet and unengaged, like shadows of their usual larger-than-life selves. Quietly, Bal, our Nepalese leader, told us there had been a fight outside the bar last night and it involved two of the team. He was in bed when he got a call from some friends in the military stationed in Namche.

The police had turned up and our guys were close to spending the night in cells before Bal intervened to sort out the situation.

"I am so upset. This is not acceptable in our culture," he said. The rest of us were open-mouthed as we digested the story, which seemed to involve fists flying between our guys and some fellow British trekkers who had apparently taken offence at them chatting to some women in their group. I could feel embarrassment, frustration and anger building inside.

When the rest of the boys staggered into breakfast, one of them was sporting a half-closed, deep purple black eye. I caught his gaze down the table.

"Why are you looking at me like that?" he fired.

"How am I looking?"

"Like you're disappointed."

"That's because I am disappointed in you. I'm really embarrassed. You've let our whole team down."

On the hike back down to Lukla I couldn't bring myself to talk to any of them but by the time we'd flown back to Kathmandu I had thawed and I sat next to black-eye boy at our last dinner together.

"I know you were disappointed, but I want to ask you Mandy, when was the last time you were ever in a fight?" he said.

I sort of laughed. "Well, I've never been in one."

"That's precisely it, isn't it? You grew up in Sale, literally thirty miles from where we grew up, and yet our upbringings couldn't be more different. Every single time since we began going to pubs as teenagers, somebody would try to pick a fight, particularly with J because he's so big. Even now, every time he goes to a pub, some young whippersnapper will try to have a pop.

"So you can't put your slant of your life, and your perception on us, because when someone comes up to me, I am not just going to stay sitting in a chair and assume that they're coming with good intent. I'm going to assume that they are coming over because they are about to hit me, so instinctively we react accordingly."

He made his point very eloquently, and though I didn't agree with him it was another lesson in judgement and perceptions based on your own life experience. Again, we are all different and have different views on the world. That goes for colleagues in the office as much as it does random people from outside your normality who you might bump into trekking to Everest. And I would say that overall, their diversity hugely added to the trip and my own personal growth.

CRAIG: Some people are good at setting big goals and then striving towards them but that's never really worked for me. I've never really had any lofty ambitions, but that's not to say the different opportunities I've had have come around by accident. My path has not been uniform. There have been many failures, plenty of ups and downs but in general it has trended in the right direction in terms of having fulfilling, interesting, different experiences in life.

I've been thoughtful about my route and plotted a course, guided by some inner sat nav I suppose, but without looking too far ahead. I totally accept and agree with Mandy's 'Dream it, believe it, do it' philosophy but I've always operated at a slightly more micro scale. What's the next thing? Shoot for the moon and you'll reach the stars, they say, well I sort of aim for the end of the road and then decide whether to turn left or right. Hopefully, I made it clear early on, that my coping mechanism is preparation.

But just as that isn't Mandy's natural state, nor is mine pinning a big target to the fridge door saying in five years' time I will be an astronaut or the drummer for Oasis, or whatever. For me, the journey should be winding with twists, turns and maybe the odd dead end. Sometime after I left EasyJet, I landed a job with an Icelandic airline named Wow Air. I went to Iceland – the country, not the frozen goods shop – and even got the uniform.

Then it went bust before I managed a single flight. Not a problem, other than no income, because I don't view life and careers as a single linear path. The point is, it is possible to not be a goal setter and still achieve good things. Are they goals? Maybe, if the scale is zoomed in and it was the project you intended to finish or the move you were angling for, but perhaps they are just the next place you've got to from where the next waypoint is unclear.

Mandy and I have both made careers in aviation, but we have flown very different routes in very different ways, which is the whole point.

Albert Einstein, another noted academic, famously wrote: 'Everybody is a genius but if you judge a fish by its ability to climb a tree it will spend its whole life believing it is stupid.'

That sort of sums up my story. Academics weren't for me, but luckily, I found a career where my limitations

Our Education System

"Everybody is a genius. But if you judge a fish by its ability to climb a tree, it will live its whole life believing that it is stupid."

weren't the focus and where other abilities were able to shine through. If I share one thing with Einstein, it's my deeply ingrained belief that everyone has unique qualities to bring to the table.

I'm all about moving forward, in life and in work. And to do that, you need to consider change. To some that might suggest I'm not content with my lot, but I would argue that you can be very content and still want to change. Viewed from the other angle, I wouldn't be content if I wasn't always looking for something new.

This doesn't have to be in terms of my career, it can be taking up drumming or trekking to Everest or volunteering at the local hospital, which has been very fulfilling.

But it would be too easy to just say you need to embrace change. Not everyone operates like that. My answer would be to consider the alternative. If you keep doing the same thing there is a real risk of complacency and stagnation.

Complacency is clearly a risk in an industry like aviation. A commercial pilot flying on the line is doing the same thing day in, day out – even though as I've stressed before, every flight is different – and I see that as a real threat. The case study of inadvertent slide deployment is a clear example of routine and complacency in action. Then there is stagnation.

I know doctors who are counting down the days until retirement. Someone else I know has worked in the same office job for his entire career because 'it offers a great pension'. True, it is just around the corner from his house, which is handy and certainly beats driving to Gatwick which is a real pain. But that whole way of thinking is just not for me.

I refuse to be like that. Nor I suspect, is it for you otherwise you wouldn't be reading this book. So, to avoid complacency and stagnation you need to change, however unsettling that might feel. I didn't particularly want to leave the navy, why would I? I got to travel, I worked with fantastic people, and it was a varied, exciting life.

But I knew I was never going to climb up the ranks and if I didn't leave, I would be bimbling about from job to job, which would have been fine. Except it wouldn't. I certainly didn't want to leave 772 Squadron flying search and rescue helicopters; it was some of the most challenging yet rewarding flying of my entire career. But I knew I wanted to keep moving and become a qualified flying instructor and that fear of stagnation was worse than the unknown that lay beyond.

Maybe it is a bit like champion sports stars who retire when they are at the very top of the game. You think, well why don't you just keep going? Everyone has different motivations, but fears of stagnation and complacency must come into it. It's a bit like getting a haircut. For a few weeks you notice it getting shaggier and you think, I really need a trim. But as time goes on you start looking at it thinking, that's actually alright, I'm owning it, I can last a bit longer. Then the moment you do get it cut, people say you look great, and you think, "So what you're really saying is I've been walking around looking like a twit". But now you feel liberated, fresher and wish you'd got it cut much sooner. With the right approach, which is looking forward and adapting, life on the other side of change will be alright.

There might be certain aspects you miss of your old state but there will be other, perhaps as yet unknown, positives with the new. Lean into those. I'm very fired up about evidence-based training and that might not have come my way had I stayed flying on the line. For me, it's not about stepping up the ladder, I want to go sideways sometimes.

It's the change that keeps me interested. I hadn't even considered writing a book, but it became an interesting and very different project.

I should make it clear; I'm not talking change for change's sake. We've all become irritated when a new senior colleague comes in and starts changing all the operating procedures just to make their mark. It can be highly frustrating when you have learned the system and it works and it feels like they are doing it for the sake of it. But equally, a closed mindset of "this is how we've always done it here" is not useful either.

If the change is framed correctly, with sound reasoning behind it, people are more likely to get on board. There was a certain amount of resistance to the extra stop-checks introduced after the inadvertent slide deployment study, but when it was explained to people why it was being implemented and what might happen if it wasn't – that they could be the one going through the motions one day and then cause a tragedy by knocking a worker off a gantry – they pretty quickly embraced it.

For the individual, if your situation is working and you are content, then no problem, crack on. But if there is a yearning for something else, an inquisitiveness about the world, people and other opportunities then consider it.

Where my desire to keep moving forward comes from is largely the loss of my brother Paul. He didn't get a chance to live his life, so I feel I have a responsibility to him and other people to live as full a life as possible. Live more, fear less!

MANDY: Near the end of a speech I was giving in Yorkshire one evening, an elderly gent raised his hand to ask a question. I was building up to my big finale and my first thought was, "No, you can't interject, I've got a really good ending, and you'll ruin it." But I thought I'd better let him say a few words and I invited his input. With a strong voice, he said he was eighty years old and had worked for the National Trust for the last thirty-eight years. Every day, he said, he had glanced at the big lawnmower sitting in the shed and dreamed of driving it.

He yearned to sit on that green, metal seat, hold the wide bars and feel the chug of the engine as he puttered up and down, crafting lush green lines in the lawn. He always thought he could do it, but something was holding him back. For thirty-eight years. But he said listening to my tales had finally convinced him and the very next day he was going to get on that lawnmower and take it for a spin.

I've since incorporated that in some of my talks. The majority of people are not dreaming of becoming fast jet pilots, but everyone will have the equivalent of their lawnmower moment. What is yours?

Recently, I was asked to speak at a special measures school in Southampton. I had tailored my talk to suit the audience and was in full flow when my eye caught a girl sitting at the front with dyed red hair, piercings everywhere and a hard, defiant face that screamed, not interested. Looks like trouble, I thought to myself as I blustered on. The following day the headteacher called me and told me a story.

She said one of her pupils, a girl in the front row at the speech – I may have noticed her – was highly intelligent but refused to go to college. The school was encouraging her to do maths, further maths and physics but she was adamant she was going to be a beautician like all her mates (no slight on beauticians at all, by the way). But apparently, she had sought out the head after my talk.

"You know what, Miss, f*** it, I've decided if she can f**king do it, so can I. I will go to college, and I will do my A'levels like you've been pushing me to do."

The headteacher wanted to quote her verbatim to explain that she didn't pull the girl up for swearing because she was so overwhelmed that someone had finally inspired her to explore her potential. Sometime later I was doing a workshop with a group of CEOs and we were going around the room asking people to say what they were most proud of. I had been speaking at a huge conference to 4,000 people the week before and this might have been the obvious thing to bring up, but as I waited for my turn to go, I realised that what I was most proud of was having some sort of effect on the girl with the F-bombs. I thought, if I can influence the direction of travel for one individual by giving a speech, then that to me is success.

MANDY AND CRAIG: Our mission brief was to add a bit of oxygen to your already smouldering desire to change your path, whether that's to spark a series of small tweaks or set you on course for bigger disruption. Hopefully, we've encouraged you to challenge yourself and given you the impetus to push out of your comfort zone to experience and open up new opportunities.

Our fictional flight has come full circle, and the wheels are safely back on the runway. Along the way we have faced into the fear of failure, pushed ourselves away from the comfort of the runway and climbed through the clouds of self-doubt and imposter syndrome. We have taken a moment to look out of the cockpit and consider how to create the right environment for ourselves and for those around us to thrive and why choosing your reaction to situations is a superpower only you have.

Turbulence is a common threat in aviation, and we used this phase of the flight to investigate the bumps and threats in our everyday life and career, issues that might put us in an Undesirable Aircraft State and hamper our future course.

In 'Buzzing the Tower', we looked at threats of our own making, where we as humans in the system create the problem. That might be channeling our inner Maverick and defying the rules, or it could be when we inadvertently make a mistake which could spiral into a bigger issue. Again, it's how we as individuals and leaders respond which is the key to smoothing our future path.

We have heard the captain speak and reflected on what leadership really means. We have explored how to make better decisions and untangle dilemmas, and discovered that sometimes there is no perfect answer, only the next best action. But we also explored leadership as we see it, and why it might not be the ultimate destination you should be striving for.

One cool part of flying is doing aerobatics. The rush of the G-force and the satisfaction of bottoming out after a smooth loop is addictive. It fits neatly as a metaphor for life, too in the sense that we all need some fun along the way to keep things interesting. We used this chapter as a way of looking at flying high and mastering our skills, using focused debriefs to improve and challenging the system, examining whether there are better ways forward.

And now we are back on the ground, ready to refuel and plan the next mission. This is the point where we hand you the controls. The flight plan from here is yours to write. Wherever you decide to go, we hope you take forward the courage to face fear, the confidence to navigate uncertainty and the curiosity to keep looking for new horizons. Now go and fly your own mission.

GLOSSARY OF TERMS

AAR
Air-to-air refuelling is the process of transferring aviation fuel from one military aircraft (the tanker) to another (the receiver) during flight.

ACARS
Aircraft Communications Addressing and Reporting System. A digital datalink system that allows aircraft to send and receive messages with ground stations or other aircraft.

ACM
Air combat manoeuvres.

AFTS
Advanced Flying Training School at RAF Valley.

ATC
Air traffic controller/Air Training Corps.

BANDIT
An aircraft identified as enemy.

BOGEY
A radar or visual air contact whose identity is unknown.

BFTS
Basic Flying Training School at RAF Linton on Ouse.

BINGO
Pre-determined fuel state for monitoring fuel consumption.

BULLDOG
British two-seat side-by-side training aerobatic aircraft.

CHAFF
Radar countermeasure in which aircraft spreads a cloud of small, thin pieces of aluminium, metallized glass

fibre or plastic, which either appears as a cluster of primary targets on radar screens or swamps the screen with multiple returns.

CHICKEN
Minimum fuel state for a recovery to base.

C IN C
Commander in Chief.

CRM
Crew Resource Management.

DIT
An amusing anecdote.

DOGFIGHT
Aerial battle between fighter aircraft conducted at close range.

EBT
Evidence based training.

FLARES
Infrared countermeasure used to counter an infrared heat-seeking surface-to-air missile. Flares are composed of a pyrotechnic composition based on magnesium or another hot-burning metal, with burning temperature equal to or hotter than engine exhaust. The aim is to make the infrared-guided missile seek out the heat signature from the flare rather than the aircraft's engines.

FLIR
Forward looking Infra-red.

FIREFLY
Two-seat aerobatic training aircraft, built by Slingsby Aviation.

FLT LT
Flight Lieutenant.

FOD
Foreign object damage.

'G'
Unit of acceleration. One 'g' equals the force of gravity.

G-SUIT
Flight suit worn pilots who are subject to high levels of g force (g). It is designed to prevent a black-out caused by the blood pooling in the lower part of the body when under acceleration.

GPS
Global Positioning System.

HARRIER
Anglo-American vertical/short take-off and landing ground attack aircraft.

HAWK
British single-engine, jet-powered advanced trainer aircraft.

HUD
Head up display.

JEFTS
Joint Elementary Flying Training School.

JUNTA
Military slang for junior aircrew.

LSJ
Life support jacket.

NBC
Nuclear Biological Chemical Warfare.

NTOCU
National Tornado Operational Conversion Unit.

NVGS
Night vision goggles.

OLF
Operational low flying.

OPS
Operations.

PAR
Precision approach radar.

PAVEWAY IV
Dual mode GPS and laser-guided 500lb bomb.

PICKLE
Weapon release.

QFI
Qualified Flying Instructor.

QWI
Qualified Weapons Instructor.

RADALT
Radar altimeter.

RAFC
Royal Air Force College Cranwell.

RHWR
Radar homing warning receiver.

SAM
Surface to air missile.

SAS
Special Air Service.

SAT NAV
Satellite Navigation.

SIDEWINDER
Aim 9L heatseeking short range air-to-air missile.

SQN LDR
Squadron Leader.

TFR
Terrain Following Radar.

TIALD
Thermal Imaging Airborne Laser Designator.

TORNADO GR4
Twin-engine, variable-sweep wing aircraft designed to excel at low-level penetration of enemy defences.

TORNADO F3
Air defence/fighter variant of Tornado.

TRANSPONDER
Electronic device that produces a response when it receives a radio-frequency interrogation.

TUCANO
Two-seat turboprop basic trainer aircraft.

UBAS
University of Birmingham Air Squadron.

UAV
Unmanned aerial vehicle.

UHF
Ultra High Frequency radio.

VHF
Very High Frequency radio.

Printed in Dunstable, United Kingdom

71829869R00150